IMAGINING
TO LEARN

IMAGINING TO LEARN

Inquiry, Ethics, and Integration Through Drama

JEFFREY D. WILHELM
University of Maine at Orono

BRIAN EDMISTON
The Ohio State University

Forewords by James A. Beane and Jessica Dvorak

HEINEMANN
Portsmouth, NH

Heinemann
A division of Reed Elsevier Inc.
361 Hanover Street
Portsmouth, NH 03801-3912

Offices and agents throughout the world

Library of Congress Cataloging-in-Publication Data
Wilhelm, Jeffrey D., 1959–
     Imagining to learn : Inquiry, ethics, and integration through drama / Jeffrey
  D. Wilhelm, Brian Edmiston.
        p. cm.
     Includes bibliographical references.
     ISBN 0-435-07041-X
     1. Drama in education.   I. Edmiston, Brian.
     PN3171.W555   1998   97-22783
     371.39'9—dc21   CIP

Editor: Lisa A. Barnett
Cover design: Darci Mehall
Manufacturing: Louise Richardson

Printed in the United States of America on acid-free paper
01 00 99   DA   2 3 4 5 6 7 8 9

For
Peggy Jo Wilhelm: A gifted teacher, generous spirit, and (please don't forget!)
terrific friend, wife, mom, and skiing partner.
—Jeff Wilhelm

For all the people with whom I've imagined and learned.
—Brian Edmiston

Contents

Foreword

The wonderful concepts and values that constitute progressive curriculum theories mean little if they are not alive in the everyday experiences of teachers and young people. For this reason, those of us who are committed to progressive pedagogy are constantly in search of new and better ways to do our classroom work. Historically, one of the best sources of ideas has been written works combining detailed accounts of classroom episodes, reflective thinking about them, and explication of the theories to which they are linked. Among the many that come to mind are Meredith Smith's *Education and the Integration of Behavior* (1927), Gertrude Noar's *Freedom to Live and Learn* (1948), and Rosalind Zapf's *Democratic Processes in the Secondary Classroom* (1959). Now we may add to that list Jeffrey Wilhelm and Brian Edmiston's account of the place of drama in a progressive curriculum, *Imagining to Learn: Inquiry, Ethics, and Integration Through Drama.*

This fascinating book intertwines several scripts, three of which I want to note here. The first script is about "drama" itself. Drama, the authors tell us, "is not theater." Rather, it is "creating meaning together and creating visible mental models of our understanding together, in imaginative contexts and situations . . . It is not about performance, but about exploration." Defining drama in this way sets the stage for a book that is about taking young people inside issues and events in ways that simultaneously make knowledge more accessible and promote significant self and social meanings.

We are helped to understand this definition through a remarkable collection of vignettes in which teachers and students work together dramatically. To understand the meaning of culture, they imagine themselves as anthropologists studying young adolescents. To explore the contradictions and tensions involved in the United States welfare debate, they imagine themselves alternately as senators voting to send welfare recipients to another planet and as welfare recipients treated as undesirable human beings. To explore protest and resistance, they "participate" in an anti-war demonstration during the Vietnam War. To examine race and civil rights, they place themselves inside the events involved in Hank Aaron's career in major league baseball.

Make no mistake, these are not simple simulations. In each of those cases, and others, the teachers and students are led by their "insider" view to confront complex and significant questions that would almost certainly be left untouched by passive modes of teaching and learning. How do adults see young adolescents as a group? What about us and what we do would strike an observer as particularly noteworthy? Does welfare involve personal failing or social inequity? Why would supporters of the Vietnam War not listen to those who argued against it? How did Hank Aaron's life change when he went to the (white) major leagues? How would his experience have been different if he were white?

In opening up these kinds of questions, important issues and the events that mark them are brought to life and treated with the depth that they deserve. In this sense, reading the many case examples of dramatic exploration, I was reminded of the response that John Dewey reputedly made when asked to consider the place of emotion in cognition: "Knowledge is but a cup of tea floating on a sea of emotion." It is clear from those examples that the use of drama holds real promise for making content more accessible to more young people. But more than that, it adds to the possibility that content will make sense to them. After all, the events and undertakings that are involved in personally and socially significant issues and concepts are not inert "things." They are the doings of real people with all that means in terms of perceptions, feelings, contradictions, tensions, and so on. To conduct any kind of serious intellectual exploration about such issues and events requires "getting inside" them to see how those affective dimensions might be at work. Put another way, the passive and detached way in which issues and events are too often studies in schools is simply an artifice. Drama, on the other hand, brings us closer to seeing both the cup of tea *and* the sea of emotion.

A second script within the book links drama with other ideas about curriculum, teaching, and learning that are decidedly and intentionally progressive. In this case, the authors take us on a grand tour of numerous aspects of progressive pedagogy, connecting drama, as they define it, to each. For example, dramatic episodes may serve as problem-centered contexts for integrating knowledge from a variety of sources. It may also serve as a design process for pursuing greater depth in project-based learning. It encourages young people to ask critical questions and to think critically in finding responses. It serves as a moment of engagement with events and issues that otherwise might seem remote. It offers a process that supports inquiry-based learning. It promotes exploration of personal and social meaning as participants imagine themselves on the inside of events. It offers a way of connecting affect and cognition as they are in life everywhere outside the typical school curriculum. And, by making knowledge more accessible, it helps bridge the gap between the broader progressive agenda and the desire for achievement of academic skills.

That a particular method could offer so much that is critical, democratic, and constructive may seem almost too good to be true. Yet, as the authors demonstrate in their many vignettes, drama has this kind of potential. Considering this broad potential we might compare drama to teacher action research in terms of the many openings that activity offers for progressive moments in teachers' lives. Leaving almost no stone unturned, in fact, the authors point out that drama is a way to bring action research into the lives of young people as they get inside issues and discover ways of acting upon them.

The third script is about what happens among teachers and students as they engage in drama. I have come to believe that many teachers and students experience continuing tension in their relationships partly because neither group finds its school role or the curriculum particularly engaging, lively, or life-like. But, as we listen to the anecdotes in this book we can sense the tension dissolving. I'm sure there are "down" days in this approach, but surely not as many as there are in most others. The teacher here plays a leading role, shaping the dramatic experience by pressing students for more depth, more information, more understanding, more insight. Yet, the teacher is a learner too, faced with the same unanswered questions as the students and pulled along by the dramatic experience toward an unpredictable end. The students are pulled out of the passive roles they have often learned to play and pressed into engaging confrontation with the puzzling and complex meanings "behind the facts" that are the usual fare in the school curriculum. Out of their usual strained roles, the teachers and students seem to find each other as people involved in a mutual conversation about issues, events, and problems.

There is one other thing I want to say by way of introducing this book, and it is perhaps more important than the rest. I am married to a highly

skilled and progressive middle school teacher and have spent a good deal
of time in recent years teaching with her using a teacher-student planned,
problem-centered curriculum. In other words, we are working with a curriculum that is more than a little sophisticated. As soon as I finished reading the book manuscript I handed it to her and suggested that here might
be something to add to our work. I can think of no better way to compli-
ment *Imagining to Learn: Inquiry, Ethics, and Integration Through Drama* than to
say that it struck me as something worth the time of a skilled and progressive teacher. In a time when we are all faced with more and more literature that is distanced from the everyday lives of teachers and students, that
bears the bad news of the conservative restoration, and that seeks to promote a mindless and disengaging curriculum, it is refreshing to have a
book that tells again how powerful progressive pedagogy can be. We need
more like it.

James A. Beane
National-Louis University

Foreword

Drama is a great way to learn. It's like reliving history. You remember what you learn much better—as something you did rather than as something you heard in school. I remember what I learned a year ago through drama more vividly than I remember last month's social studies. I wish schools used drama. There are many good things about it, such as the way it makes learning easier and how it needs no textbooks. It's easy to relate to whatever you are studying. That helps everyone get involved. I like drama a lot.

I enjoyed the workshops on castles that I went to last year. I learned a lot about castles, how they are preserved, their history, and museums. I remember almost everything, too! However, if you asked me about the Revolutionary War, which I studied just six or seven weeks ago, I would not remember much. It took effort on all our parts to make the workshop a success. We had research to do, artifacts to make and bring in, and problems to solve. Learning is not always easy, but it does not have to be boring. That workshop made it fun.

Drama helps you understand people's actions—especially the thoughts and feelings that led to those actions. We do not learn history just so that we will know a lot about something that happened hundreds or thousands of years ago. We study history to learn from the mistakes others have made. Through drama, we can find out what led to those mistakes and how we can prevent similar incidents from happening again. If every person in the world knew what the victims of the Holocaust thought and felt, would there be another Holocaust?

I doubt it. We need to learn more from the past than dates and names. Drama is a great way to learn.

Jessica Dvorak

Acknowledgments

I know exactly where I ought to start the acknowledgments for this book: with Brian Edmiston. There's not much in my teaching life (and certainly not much in this book) that Brian has not influenced. Brian is an incredibly generous teacher who has that very human gift of rapport with whomever he works. Thanks, Brian!

Of course, how could I have ever taught in the ways described in this book without the support and tremendous energy provided by Paul Friedemann, my team teaching partner for many years at Beaver Dam Middle School? I couldn't have. Paul liked to joke that we were the Lennon and McCartney of nontraditional curriculum. Certainly we enjoyed a synergistic enthusiasm and had the panache to try out whatever we felt would promote the learning of our students. We certainly made just about as much noise (we'd call it 'music') as our students did during our drama, hypermedia, and video documentary work. This was often pointed out to us by teachers in neighboring classrooms.

For that matter, thanks to all of my colleagues throughout the years who supported innovative work and who were willing to converse and experiment with me. Experimenting with new notions of teaching, learning, and schooling is no small risk, and it's good to have great company to work with. Most notably, I want to thank my friends Judy Bovee, Brian Ambrosius, Nancy Cook, Craig Martin, Erv Barnes, and Jackie Burke. There are many others as well, and you know who you are. Thanks!

Thanks to Rand Harrington, who has helped me to see the use of drama, physical modeling, and re-enactments in the field of science education. Rand is a great colleague and fills the void left by Paul both on and off the basketball court. Steve Kaback has also helped me to understand teaching content in the sciences. Thanks to you, Steve.

I'd be remiss in not thanking Peter Smagorinsky, who was the first to encourage me to start writing about drama. His own work in this area helped me see how to do so.

And I must mention my new colleagues at the University of Maine, who are tremendously smart, supportive, and friendly. I have counted on their continual kindnesses and sophisticated insights as thinkers, teachers, and readers. Thanks along these lines go to Brenda Power, Jan Kristo, Paula Moore, Phyl Brazee, Ed Brazee, and Rosemary Bamford. As a group, I'd say they know more about teacher research, children's literature, middle level education, and teaching as assisted performance as any group I've ever known or can imagine knowing.

Thanks to my father, Jack Wilhelm, a courageous and forward-looking educator. And I'm always filled with gratitude for the support of my wife, Peggy Jo, music educator, mother, and wife extraordinaire.

Thanks also to my own secondary school teachers Bill Strohm and James Blaser. Their own magnificent teaching inspired me to teach. Thanks is always due to my great friend and mentor, Michael W. Smith, who started me off on this phase of my teaching journey by eliciting my beliefs, confronting them, and then confronting them some more. Michael surely knows how to push students through the zone of proximal development! But then, like all of these folks, he's a teacher.

A big thank you to all!

Jeffrey Wilhelm

I tried writing conventional acknowledgments but I found the form constricting. Instead, I have created extracts from notes which I could have written to some of those who have enriched my life and been fellow travelers on my journey as a teacher who uses drama.

Dear Dorothy (Heathcote):

After 14 years I am still weaving your insights into my teaching. I wanted to let you know that you're mentioned throughout a book which I am . . .

E-mail to Cecily O'Neill:
See you in Ohio or London! I've just reread the *Drama Worlds* manuscript and it captures the aesthetic complexity of your drama teaching yet also speaks clearly to teachers who . . .

Note to Gavin Bolton:
Thank you for your insights on that teaching strategy. I was wondering how your ideas about constraint would have . . .

Graduation congratulations to a former student:
Though it has been years since we shared a classroom, I wanted to thank you for your trust and tolerance as I learned with you about the power of imagination. Do you remember everyone laughing when I said that I felt I was the student . . .

Birthday card to Michael (7) or Zoë (3):
The day of your birth was a glorious day, equaled only by the day we first started playing together . . .

E-mail to Jeff:
Yes, let's go skiing this weekend. I am so glad you kept notes today in your classroom!! About your idea for a book—I know you'll have the energy to keep me at it, so let's keep talking . . .

E-mail to a colleague:
Thank you for the feedback. I was so glad that you pointed out . . .

Handwritten note to Pat Enciso (partners in parenting and education):
I went in to the office at 4:00—I will be back in time for breakfast. Thanks for your comments. Could you send me an E-mail . . .

diary entry to myself:
Remember that all days weren't like this—don't forget last week when those kids sang and didn't want to go to recess. You know that if you keep at it competence will come in time.

Brian Edmiston

Introduction

JEFFREY WILHELM

If you want to know what this book is about, let me be direct: If you are interested in "teaching," that is, in creating an environment that will stimulate, support, and guide ever more competent performances of knowledge and skill, if you want to provide the instruction and context necessary for students to grow in ever more sophisticated understandings of how the world works, then this book is for you. In it, Brian and I argue that drama is a natural and uniquely powerful form of teaching abstract concepts from fields of history, science, and math, as well as the communicative arts. We also argue that drama is a unique and powerful way to support reading, to educate the imagination, to inform our values. Drama is a potent mode of both student- and teacher-conducted research, as well as a device that naturally integrates instruction in ways that progressive education reformers have long advocated. In this way, drama can be a means of reforming the curriculum.

Because of this, we believe that every teacher, at every grade level, in every subject area, no matter his or her background, needs to make drama a part of the teaching repertoire. Drama is a fundamentally human way of engaging with and exploring the world. This is what our book is about. The rest is evidence, story, detail, argument, and illustration.

From the very start of my own teaching career, I noticed the extraordinary power of drama activities to engage my students and to support their thinking in new ways.

Most of my career has been spent teaching students who wore labels, like millstones, around their neck. Each year of my fifteen years of teaching I've taught mainstreamed classes full of students with warning stickers attached, such as learning disabled (LD), attention deficit disorders or emotionally/behaviorally disturbed. I've also taught countless kids who were reluctant, if not resistant, readers and learners. Yet all of these kids seemed to love drama and demonstrated that they, like more successful students, found drama activity an exciting and natural way to comprehend difficult and often very abstract networks of ideas.

When I taught tenth grade, I remember pursuing a simulation of Puritan life. Three boys labeled LD, who were indeed most definitely behavior problems, immediately volunteered for the three major roles of preacher, teacher, and judge. Throughout the two-week simulation, they wrote journals, kept elaborate records of our "village life," and prepared for town meetings. They planned each day thoroughly and performed their roles flawlessly, often refusing to give up the simulation when they left the classroom. I could see them hand out "letters of shame" in the lunchroom to classmates drinking soda or engaging in other "unseemly" behaviors. Some of their classmates complained that they were taking the unit *too seriously!* The classes then role-played with great delight and intensity through *The Crucible*, a play that had thrown the previous year's students with an absolute "hissy-fit," as one girl told me.

Even so, in these first years of teaching, I had only begun to scratch the surface of dramatic possibilities for engaging students and supporting their learning. For me, this book is about what happened and what followed for me after I met Brian Edmiston, as he guided my use of drama in more wide-awake and powerful ways. I was never trained in drama or theater, never had course work in either, and had only minimal personal experience with the medium, except as a member of an appreciative audience. Brian showed me that *drama is not theater*. Drama is creating meaning and visible mental models of our understanding together, in imaginative contexts and situations. It is not about performance, but exploration. And the teacher in drama becomes a learner among learners, a participant, and a guide, who lends expertise to the students.

This book concerns the power of drama to teach. This teaching is at once personal, social, ethical, substantive, and content-oriented. The stories we tell here include both research stories that happened in real classrooms and arguments that drama can, and should, be used across the curriculum as a natural and powerful way to understand ideas, to come to terms with other perspectives, to try out new ways of being and thinking, to learn how to learn, and to learn how to assist others in their learning.

I'd like to highlight here a couple of themes about teaching that drama helped me to discover. First, I've come to think of teaching as assisted performance. As has been pointed out by various researchers and commentators, teachers in schools in the United States rarely do much teaching—they assign and they evaluate. To guide and assist ever more competent learning performances means to involve oneself in the process of learning, in helping students at the point of need in their struggle to create new understandings. Drama is a powerful way of doing this because it makes students' current understandings visible, and because it provides a medium in which to manipulate and try out new possibilities. When done well, this risk-taking environment is exciting, challenging, full of risks, but safe. Not only can I assist my students in greater learning in the context of the drama, but the dramatic context provides real and very human reasons for learning. The drama work often also becomes art, and provides a powerful aesthetic experience for the students who create it.

Drama always allows the students to assist me as a teacher as they reveal, in their roles, what they know, what they find difficult, and what they need to know next. Especially exciting to me is that the various dramas I have pursued over the years provided a fresh start for *all* of my students, and situations in which students took on roles of authority, and in which they assisted each other to go beyond their current understandings and to outgrow their current selves. Many students, like Sean, left drama sessions with a comment like, "Wow, intense! That was *really* something!" or "Whoa, I'm tired! That's more work than gym class!"

Along the same lines, Brian has done a lot over the years to assist my performance as a content-area teacher using drama to serve the learning goals of the curriculum. He has assisted by coming into my classroom and modeling his use of drama as a team-teacher. He has done it by coaching and commenting from the back of the classroom, and he has assisted my performance through conversation over the telephone and E-mail, by responding to student artifacts and to my own stories.

It occurs to me that this kind of collaboration rarely occurs in education. It's certainly been rare in my experience, even though I've spent several years teaching on an integrated team. Even in team teaching, it's been rare that one of us had pedagogical expertise to lend to the other, or that teammates took the opportunity to groom and support each other carefully over time in the development of a new way of teaching. What Brian did for me, coming from the university to work with me and my students, sometimes most of the day for a week or two at a time, seems to occur only rarely.

Now, for me, things seem to have come full circle. Learning leads to more learning; collaboration seems to beget greater collaboration. Drama has become a natural and continual part of my teaching repertoire, whether I am teaching middle school reading or science, or whether I am teaching a literature or research course at the university. When I do dramas, I often bring in local experts to help us set them up, to offer a critique of the understandings we are creating, or to participate with us. Like the kids, these local experts seem—even if initially hesitant—to take to drama as a natural, fun, and powerful way to learn.

Now that I am at the university, I am actively helping six teachers in six different schools to use drama in various content areas, often with very recalcitrant students. The story has always been the same. The teachers are hesitant; the kids may initially resist. But after a couple of sessions, everyone is engaged and the kids are asking to learn by using the techniques of drama.

This book is an attempt to move drama into the mainstream of teaching, learning, and curriculum development here in the United States. It is an argument and a demonstration that drama is a powerful form of assisting student performance. It is a way of setting parameters by which students can help construct curriculum and pursue personally relevant yet socially significant projects. Further, it is a method of assessment and of teacher research that makes learning visible. Finally, drama methods consist of a flexible set of strategies that support student reading and help them to learn sophisticated and highly abstract content and to explore values and forge new understandings. Drama helps students to "see" what they are reading and learning, to create mental models and coherent networks of thought, to apply, and to play out possibilities and consequences in a secure setting.

Drama needs to be a part of every teacher's repertoire, in every content area, and at every grade level. It can be easily introduced to students and can be used successfully even by teachers who initially resist it. Our stories here should clearly demonstrate that fact, and it is hoped, they will help you on your way to doing it too.

Happy reading!

BRIAN EDMISTON

If I could no longer use drama, I would become an impoverished teacher. Drama releases imagination and creates opportunities for learning unlike any other medium. With students of any age, in school or college classrooms and with my children at home, creating drama worlds has become integral to engagement, dialogue, assessment, sharing, and exploration of topics.

I wasn't always so passionate about using drama in the classroom. As a young middle- and high-school teacher in England I had been instructed "not to smile before Christmas" and to keep students "on task." So, I dutifully adopted my peers' controlling style that kept students reading literature and studying history mostly in silence and alone, but rarely with deep or enthusiastic engagement. Drama meant performance and was a frill which we *might* get to on Friday if our work was completed. I could not understand why students were not as interested as I was in the issues that were embedded in the texts we read—I did not realize that for most students, texts never came to life. I struggled to bring the worlds of books alive through discussion, games, and innovative strategies. I even closed my classroom door and tried acting out scenes. I had only very marginal success—words and content were more often barriers than windows into human experiences. Drama seemed to promote frivolity rather than depth of experience.

The students' attitudes to the text—and to me—radically altered when in desperation I created authentic-looking historical documents based on the stories of an infamous eighteenth-century local gang. When students became juries and witnesses in trials of the gang, suddenly they *wanted* to read, write stories, debate, create evidence, enact past events, and critique other viewpoints. The curriculum of enthusiasm which I had envisioned as unattainable dramatically materialized in the classroom. While students bounded into class demanding that I help them write a judicial sentence, create an old-looking diary entry, or enact a deportation, I searched for a teacher from whom I could learn how to harness this energy. Fortunately I found Dorothy Heathcote, enrolled myself in her year-old master's program, and discovered that I had stumbled into a use of drama in which students work together to imagine in order to learn.

I did not anticipate that our first teaching assignment would be to engage students with the Christmas story in a hospital for the severely physically and mentally disabled. I initially felt that I could hardly relate to students who included autistic children and wheelchair-bound geriatrics. However, as our week's work unfolded I had a profound realization about teaching—I had to try to see the world as particular students viewed it and in doing so would draw out our human commonalities, rather than stress our differences. In drama, these students could experience the significance of the arrival of a "wise person" and they could do so much more through the rhythm of drums, the placing of a crown of tinsel, and our gestures of bowing, than they could in words alone.

I was discovering core principles of drama in education: meanings are created in interaction, carefully created images engage and show ideas, and that despite any "disabilities," teachers strive to be respectful and equal partners in learning with students. Most of all, I realized that we must accept students as they are before we can begin to show them alternatives.

In working with teachers and students of all ages and all years of experience and teaching styles, I have come to believe that anyone can use drama to inquire into any curricular area. You will be more successful, however, if you value: playing with ideas, genuine dialogue, and learning in reflection.

Playing with ideas leads us to see texts and content from multiple viewpoints—perspectives that can be enacted in drama. In doing so, we recognize that understanding events is always more complex and sophisticated than we at first believe. How was the arrival of Columbus viewed by native people in 1492, by poor Spanish peasants, by his royal patrons, and by different groups in 1892 or 1992? Drama can help students begin to consider these questions and also address abstract issues like representation, evidence, and justice in specific contexts and with depth of experience and precise viewpoints that are almost impossible to sustain in ordinary discussion. Further, in our play with ideas, we can use the art form of drama to create new views, new perspectives, and alternative visions of the past, present, and future.

Genuine dialogue is more than conversation—it means shared ownership of the curriculum and making meaning together. It creates spaces where students *and* teachers are open to different ideas and alternative viewpoints. Drama contains the seeds of classroom democracy. Engaging with students' challenging questions and ideas becomes as important as encountering positions taken from texts. In drama, students' real-world questions become relevant. If people protested genocide, why did it not stop? Could we have behaved differently? How does this relate to what's happening in the world today? How do you write history that is fair? Drama can bring questions like these to life in spaces where participants are protected into a respectful sharing of different views. Drama can revitalize a dead or dying curriculum with heated dialogue and the breath of fresh ideas.

Reflection is the key to learning. Without reflection, we will never learn from our "mis-takes" to become better teachers. Unless we reflect, no one has a chance of reconsidering past views, creating new understandings, or empathizing with others. In drama, students can begin to recognize that although views have been socially and culturally constructed, people need not be either passive receivers of meanings or wholly victims of circumstance. Reflection in drama allows students to think and feel from within other points of view and to forge meanings from multiple perspectives—meanings that are not parroted opinions but authentic positions.

We know that students will never care about any subject area—from history to science—until they ask themselves the sorts of authentic questions which professionals ask. We know that schools are filled with students who do not care about learning the "3 Rs" because they do not feel a need to learn them, or who struggle over a book report because the book has never come alive for them.

We hope that this book comes alive for you. It is filled with examples of how drama can create contexts that open up students' energies, abilities, and questions; contexts in which students can discover a reason to read, a need to think, and a community that cares about their ideas.

Drama is as natural as laughter and is at the core of our humanity. Drama is shared imagination in action; it is the showing and making of ideas in interaction. Just as our three year old daughter Zoë uses drama to transform destructive dragons into sharing friends, so can teachers and students together transform sterile classrooms into spaces where people are "imagining to learn."

IMAGINING
TO LEARN

1

Exploring Castles:
Authentic Teaching
and Learning through Drama

Brian Edmiston and Jeffrey D. Wilhelm

I've been asking lots of questions. Asking what might people have been doing, think-ing and feeling because they were here [in the castle]. I wondered a lot too. I wondered what their lives were like and why people were here and what might have happened to them if they were outside. . . . I used the things we found [artifacts and written mate-rials] and tried to figure out what they meant, how they were used, that kind of stuff. I thought a lot about women and how they have been treated and how they could get things done for themselves throughout history. I got the chance to experiment with those questions and to do and feel the things those castle people did for myself. I don't know what historians do, but that's what I did during the drama.

—Jessica, grade 6

When Jessica said these words at the end of a week-long study of "Castles," I know that my eyes sparkled. I was glad that Jeff was keeping notes because I knew that I intended to repeat her words the next time I was asked by a teacher—or an administrator—what drama had to do with education. Drama had been the core of teaching and learning in our short study of European medieval society. Jessica had articulated that she had achieved our primary aim. As she imagined and worked with others, she had been thinking like an historian.

Jessica was one of ten sixth-grade students with whom I worked as an integral part of a week-long class for a dozen teachers at the University of Maine concerning the use of drama in the elementary and secondary classroom.

I was delighted that Jessica and the other students, none of whom had ever before used drama for learning, had so vividly demonstrated the power of classroom drama in the 1996 university summer institute which Jeff codirected. I remember on the first day having had to work hard to create conditions in which the students felt comfortable enough to talk, share, ask questions, or leave the security of their chairs. By the end of the week, however, they had collaboratively designed a museum, created interactive displays, danced, written a ballad, sung, and talked in depth about issues like fairness and representation.

The students' dramatizations and interactions about castles and the people who might have lived in them had evoked the world of the Middle Ages; yet these images had been created in the barren atmosphere of a college classroom devoid of established friendship groups, school library, or extensive supplies. Students and teachers worked together throughout the week. The students' enthusiasm and collaboration with each other and with the teachers, as well as the growth in their engagement over four days gave credence to the stories Jeff and I told the teachers about the previous year when Jeff had been a middle-level classroom teacher in Wisconsin and I had been a professor at the University of Wisconsin—Madison. We talked about the power of drama in the year when I had been a guest teacher in his literature-rich small-town classroom. For Jeff's students, working cooperatively in integrated units of inquiry had become the norm; over that year drama had become integral to classroom learning and teaching. Working with the students in Maine showed the teachers how communities of inquiry could be established in their classrooms and the significance of drama for the process.

I did not need to lecture the Maine teachers about current educational issues and concerns with authentic pedagogical approaches—they were demonstrated in embryo that week. Curriculum integration, student-centered inquiry in a caring community, connections with the world outside the classroom, cooperative learning, group work, critical thinking, creativity, in-depth analysis of content, arts-based learning, accommodating different learning styles, exploring related ethical concerns, and other modes all occurred in contexts in which teachers stretched students' thinking and assisted students to question ideas and to create rich, multilayered understandings. Drama enabled all of this and more.

We did not just study *history*—the students' (and the teachers') questions about the past were examined and explored in rich integrated contexts that connected the past with the present. Students read, wrote, did mathematical calculations, and planned science experiments as they thought about the history of a castle. They became deeply engaged and wanted to work together because their inquiries were rooted in their questions and because they felt safe and respected. They were not given watered down sources, but used adult references on castles. They did sit and write on occasion, but they were neither tied to a desk nor required to be silent; as appropriate, they moved and they talked. That week they also drew, sculpted, made models, danced, and sang. Deep social and ethical questions arose about medieval life—the role of women, the relative positions of rich and poor, the rights of the oppressed to rebel. In the exploration of these questions, by students and teachers together, multilayered historical, cultural, and social contexts were created that gave texture to the facts the students already knew and recently uncovered, as well as deepened the realizations and discoveries they made during our work.

This all became possible through the use of drama. Not the performance of plays or the acting out of stories, but the sort of drama in which students together imagine in order to learn. Students imagined that they were the sort of people who cared about castles—historians, archaeologists, preservationists—and for four days they saw the world through other eyes and wondered about the sorts of questions such professionals ask. As they wondered, they inquired, read, wrote, argued, thought, moved, and dramatized their ideas. As students wondered, teachers wondered with them and helped them to push their thinking and to delve into content and ideas in depth and breadth. We not only explored the physical towers and dungeons of castles in imagination; through imagination we also explored the medieval world as we studied, discovered, and created historical, cultural, social, and individual meanings associated with one particular castle.

Drama not only enabled all this, but also created a learning environment that during the week became increasingly multifaceted, supportive, and complex—a space where laughter intermingled with serious discussion, a place to which students and teachers wanted to return, and a site where imagination was harnessed in pursuit of work of quality and dignity that examined and explored issues of human concern.

WHAT IS "DRAMA"?

At its simplest, drama is wondering, "What if . . .?" and then interacting with others in a "drama world" (Edmiston 1991; O'Neill 1995), as if that imagined reality was actual. The dramatic play of three-year-old children and the theatrical performances of professional actors are created and experienced in similar aesthetic and dramatic spaces—in the realm of what the Russian director Konstantin Stanislavsky called "the magic if" (Wolf, Edmiston and Enciso, 1997).

Asking "What if . . .?" is not an optional question in the curriculum—imagining possibilities is at the core of understanding other people, other times, and other places. Imagination is an integrative force in the curriculum as students wonder: What if we were historians, kings, or serfs? What if we lived somewhere else, in the future, or in the past? What if we were older, more expert, or more powerful? What if we were younger, less experienced, or more vulnerable? When students *connect* their experiences with those of others', then their views of others and of themselves will be changed. Dorothy Heathcote, the renowned British educator and pioneer of the use of drama in the classroom, puts it like this: in drama you "put yourself in other people's shoes and by using personal experience to help you to understand their point of view you may discover more than you knew when you started" (Heathcote *et al.* 1984).

Drama in the classroom is broadly of two types that parallel the drama of the theatre and the drama of children's play: the performance of written texts and the scriptless kinds of drama in which the improvised process is the product. If students watch or perform plays, as they hear or speak the words of characters, they can consider situations from the characters' different points of view. Similarly, students who imagine that they are other people see the world from other viewpoints as they interact as if they were others. In this book, we are mostly concerned with *process* kinds of drama. When we mention "drama," unless specified otherwise, we are considering drama in which there is no external audience, no prepared script, and in which the teacher frequently takes on roles with students (Wolf, Edmiston and Enciso, 1997).

Drama harnesses students' imagination to breathe life into the concepts and content of the curriculum. As Cecily O'Neill puts it, drama "generates and embodies significant meanings and raises significant questions" (O'Neill 1995, 153). Students imagine the viewpoints of people who care about real-life concepts and content—people whose lives and concerns are too easily forgotten when teachers cover areas of the curriculum. Facts and information become relevant when they are relevant to the lives of the people the students imagine. Further, students encounter facts and concepts in context and create meaning as they interact in situations. Students are self-motivated when they imagine together in drama—when they see through others' eyes they see the curriculum from inside out. The questions that arise provide students with their own entry points into further study and indicate to teachers those directions to pursue with the class with or without the use of drama.

Teachers can focus their work through drama on any aspect of the curriculum. When students are engaged in drama, teachers and students learn about complex concepts and substantive content as they imagine themselves people concerned with relevant issues and problems. Further, since students' understandings and questions are made visible in the talk and movement of drama interactions, teachers can assess and later address students' misconceptions or confusions.

Attitudes that tend to dismiss other times, other people, or unfamiliar ideas and difficult concepts as "boring" or "irrelevant" are challenged by the *students themselves* in drama as they begin to imagine other viewpoints and situations in which the significance of abstract concepts like "justice," "truth," or "history" can come to life in the actions, concerns, and interactions of specific people in particular moments of their lives. When you have imagined a castle and yourself as a "just" king or as a minstrel telling the "truth," then your views of the "history" of medieval society are personalized and rescued from dehumanizing abstractions. Because drama experiences occur in fictional *worlds* when students imagine they are elsewhere, their *feelings* (which may never be shared) and their *movements* (which may only be seen as a tilt of the head) connect with and amplify their *thoughts* of other people, times, and places. Drama worlds are suffused with empathy because they "exist in the hearts, heads, voices, and hands of children and their teachers." As scholars from Dewey to Vygotsky have argued, "Rather than separate intellect from affect, drama, like life, weaves the two together—integrating mind and emotion within the experience and action of specific situations" (Wolf, Edmiston and Enciso, 1997).

Drama needs more than individual imagination; drama worlds are created and experienced in *interaction*. With or without the teacher, students may interact in whole group, small groups, or in pairs. Using drama in the classroom opens up the possibility of cooperative intense processes of discovery, creation, and learning. Together, the group collaboratively explores events, ideas, and themes through physical, intellectual, and emotional engagement with experiences, roles, and situations brought to life through their collective imagination.

Teacher-student interaction is crucial in drama. Although drama work follows students' interests and suggestions, the teacher is responsible for sequencing tasks and shaping the drama. Even though students will often work in small groups, it is in the *teachers'* interactions with students where ideas are most likely to be clarified, shaped, extended, and revised.

Students are not only in "role" in drama, they are "framed" (1) as people who are *responsible* for other people and who have a *need* to relate to particular content areas and ideas. If they become engaged in the drama world, their position facilitates development of a growing sense of responsibility and of significance. As trustees and curators of a proposed museum, our students in Maine were charged with a responsibility both to design a museum that would be historically accurate and appropriately engaging for future visitors.

In drama, students not only adopt positions: they encounter situations and points of view—represented by other students, texts, and by the teacher—that challenge and change them and their views of whatever they are studying. Heathcote (BBC 1971) has described drama succinctly as "a real man in a mess." The "mess" is an experience of a problem, difficulty, or dilemma. In the study of castles, students dealt with problems like designing a museum, difficulties like deciding how to explain European medieval life to contemporary Americans listening to NPR, and dilemmas like how to represent a legend accurately when so many versions of the "truth" existed.

In *dealing* with a "mess," students' views change because "drama is human beings confronted by situations which change them because of what they must face in dealing with those challenges" (Heathcote 1984, 44). What they are faced with are alternative points of view from which to make meaning, see significance, and from which to make ethical decisions.

Students' understandings are changed and become more complex as they reflect on their shifting viewpoints (Edmiston 1991a). The Russian theorist Mikhail Bakhtin argues that we only form new understandings when our viewpoint is "doubled" and we experience two or more views *at the same time* (Bakhtin 1981, 1986). Without shifts in our positions we are left to do no more than repeat the ideas of others. A doubling of viewpoints occurs more easily in art than in life; it happens repeatedly in drama as a kind of "double consciousness"—an experience of two spaces and two perspectives at once. At the same time as participants experience the actual classroom interactions among teacher and students, they also experience and interact *as if* they are elsewhere. In this drama space, their understandings change if they begin to relate: what is to what might be, the here and now to the there and then, and the self to the other (2).

Meg was one of the students whose understandings changed. At the end of our four days together, she concluded that "We never *really* know, we just think based on the little things we do know." She continued: "We have different answers because people believe differently. Museums usually only have one point of view but we have many because anything could have happened and there would be different views because there were lots of different people involved who were treated different . . . nothing's too clear cut, that's what I learned, all of these [conflicting viewpoints] might have been correct in different ways."

THE CASTLE DRAMA

My main purpose in working with the students in Maine was to show teachers how drama could create an integrated curriculum and transform study of a specific curricular area, like history, from an obsession with dates and facts to a commitment to inquiry. In addition, I wanted to demonstrate facets of the constructed, situated, connected, and ethical dimensions of learning.

The unit also had specific aims related to historical concepts. Through drama, the students explored the relevance of history and core historical concepts and preoccupations, including the following: historical questions are asked by contemporary professionals; the past may only be accessed from incomplete clues in the present that can be interpreted in different ways; past stories get retold and combined by different tellers and writers to make different "histories"; stories are told from different points of view; not all stories get retold; stories change over time. Most of all, I wanted the teachers to see that through drama the students could begin to think like historians and recognize the need for a historical viewpoint.

The students had free rein in choosing the particular historical topic. For about fifteen minutes on the first day, the students generated a list of possibilities that were narrowed down to two choices: "the Titanic" and "Castles." After a debate about why they wanted to study each, they reached a consensus on Castles.

On the next day as the students entered, they encountered drawings and diagrams of castles, medieval artifacts, and people of the Middle Ages. David Macaulay's *Castle* and *National Geographic* articles were the main sources. I asked the students to walk around, look closely at the images that we had placed on the floor and consider what interested them in the pictures. After a brief sharing, I asked them to choose one image and suggested: "If you were somebody who was interested in the history of this castle, what would you wonder about?" Students then worked in pairs, traded their pictures, and for about ten minutes shared their wonderings.

Students asked these questions and many more: How did the builders choose where to build the castle? How many stones were used to build the castle? How did they lift the stones? What machines did they have? What did they use for a water supply? How did they know the wells were safe?

Was it healthy to live in the castle? How long could inhabitants survive a siege? Who lived here and why? What about bathrooms? Why did the king live in the top story? How did the king become king? What could the people do if they didn't like the king? Why was the castle built? Why did the people serve the king? Who were the enemies of the castle? How long did the castle take to build? What was it made of? Did they have cement? Could it burn down? Why were the windows and towers built the way they were? What weapons did they use? What caused the castle to fall into ruins? What did the people eat? Is the word "villein" related to "villain"? "Cotters" to "cottages"? Were there schools? What could you do to improve your social standing? What legends and stories are there about this castle?

These were authentic questions—all were generated by the students and arose from what interested them. They had also begun to see through the eyes of "those who were interested in the history of the castle." Each question provided rich, problem-oriented, student-centered, integrated, and inquiry-driven curricular possibilities. The questions cut across subject areas such as science, math, health, history, and language arts. These historically situated questions also had connections to current social issues (from water supplies to work) and social problems (from weapons to leadership). Jim Beane (1994, 126) reminds us that curriculum materials should be generated from student interests, should be presented as "problematic" and not "authoritative," should provide possibilities for mastering important learning processes and significant content, and should connect to the social concerns of the world. Our drama work, as will be seen, allowed us to address all of these concerns.

Many of the students' questions and interactions were in the present tense, which suggested that they were beginning to imagine a fictional castle. Soon they were able to transition to interacting in a *shared* drama world. Once they had established that the castle was in England and they agreed with my suggestion that it would be interesting for them to think about turning it into a museum, I asked them to agree to take on an "expert" role.

I used the mantle of the expert drama approach and asked the students if they could imagine that they were people who worked for the [British] National Trust—they agreed (3). In mantle of the expert drama, students are cast in functional roles as knowledgeable and skillful experts whose help and advice has been requested by a client. Students initially make various joint policy decisions and engage in a series of mostly small-group short-term tasks. Even though we only worked for about eight hours over four days and students had only limited opportunities to pursue their inquiries, the mantle of the expert approach can sustain involved work over several weeks or even months.

The situation that I invented and offered as a beginning point was that the Trust had just received a gift of castle ruins on the Cornish coast. Our job: to decide when and how best to make the ruin into a museum. We reminded students that we would certainly want to address the questions they had previously generated as we pursued our drama work.

After their initial agreement I asked what professionals might work for the Trust. They gave a variety of responses including archaeologists, museum curators, trustees, and historians. Then I put them into pairs as a trustee and an archaeologist. They imagined that they "toured" the grounds of the castle during an archaeological dig looking carefully for remains of medieval artifacts. The artifacts they "found" and then shared were based on the drawings and photographs that they had just been studying so intently. Later, while the trustees slept (students lay or sat on the floor), the students who had been in role as archaeologists were free to roam the room as figures in the trustees' "dreams" of the artifacts—their whisperings and movements suggested daily doings and historical events that had occurred within the castle walls. The students began to weave historical contexts for the objects—swords had been used to kill and defend, jewelry had been worn by royalty but also by poor peasants when it had been stolen. They left for home talking about their work and, unprompted, many began their own independent research.

Most of the students arrived for the next day of our work with the fruits of their self-initiated research. One girl brought a sword she had made, a boy carried a Lego castle model, and several students brought stories and pictures of castles. All were eager to share their findings—some became a focus for that day's dramatic episodes.

As the trustees met to "debate" the purpose of the site and how to make it interesting to the public, Pat proposed creating a theme park. Kelsey and others were opposed; they suggested a living history museum and after discussion everyone agreed that this would be more appropriate. The group considered how to make the site interesting and unique. Pat argued that "it should be for kids, and for students, but have something for parents too— so people will come for school trips and on vacations." An "advertising" campaign was discussed, as was how this site would be different from other castle sites in England. The talk continued on to the ethical issues and responsibilities of a museum. When I asked, "Must our museum be true to history?" Jessica answered "Yes, but we don't know much so we'll have to try to find out more and then be true to what we know. But we'll be able to make up other things that fit with what we know, things like real people's names and games they played and things like that." This provoked further discussion about truth and history and how we come to know and be sure of things. A policy decision was made about what kind of information should be presented in the museum—it had to fit what we knew of the castle and the era but it would not be limited to actual artifacts.

The students were fascinated by the sword that Meg had made and brought in. I suggested that as the museum curators, we should discuss the creation of an "exhibit" surrounding the sword that had been discovered and of which a replica had been made. To help the students imagine a historical sword and context, I held Meg's sword reverentially and walked past the students who looked at it and each added one imaginary detail about the original ancient sword: it was heavy . . . gashed . . . jeweled . . . had a faint inscription . . . the inscription was in a different language . . . it began "Only she. . .", there were notches on the hilt . . . the handle was encrusted with gold . . . a woman's hair was braided onto the handle.

The students were intrigued by the possible implications of this inscribed sword. As the trustees, they discussed what they could find out from these details of the sword. Were the words in Cornish, French, or some other language? What would this tell us about the age and original owner of the sword? What about the gold and the notches—what did these details reveal? What did the inscription and the woman's hair mean? Could this sword have been dedicated to a knight's lady? Could it have possibly been owned by a woman? The words on the blade could be Anglo-Saxon, French, or Cornish—each would suggest a different historical era. If the castle had been King Arthur's, what language would be on the sword? Gender issues, stimulated by the detail about the woman's hair, led to a consideration of the feudal system and the roles of women in the Middle Ages and today. Students volunteered to go that night to the library to research possible answers, which were shared the next day.

Richie's model castle provided the focus for the next episode when the students suggested life-size historically accurate models of castle rooms in a visitor's center. They looked at the Lego model as well as the pictures of castles and then placed themselves throughout the room as if they were in different parts of a full-size model. As they described what could be added, Molly thought the exhibit needed to be interactive; Richie wanted it to be multimedia with sounds, music, dialogue, *a slide show* and real people playing the parts of feudal characters. The students immediately agreed. They also decided that sharing the *stories* of the people were just as important as the *facts* though the difference should be made quite clear to visitors.

Jeff now held the sword and walked around as the students improvised a draft of an evocative *tape*, which visitors would hear. A *choral montage* ensued that went as follows: Yes, sire . . . I'm hungry . . . a copper or two for the baker's dozen . . . Stitch up my boots! . . . You knave! . . . Prepare for battle! . . . Vengeance on you, you foul fiend! . . . Die! . . . I need bread! . . . Fetch me my cloak! . . . You cannot catch me . . . Play us a lay on your lyre! . . . Tell me a story . . . Let us juggle! Juggle the apples! . . . Where is my ruby necklace? . . . Drat my stew . . . I give thee my prize cow . . . Welcome, all, especially you my lord the King!

We asked the students and teachers to face away from each other (to aid concentration) and imagine that they were the historical people who had said the words they had voiced in our choral poem. We suggested that they revise or expand what they had said, to give it greater mood and dynamics—to make the tape more engaging for visitors. Jeff and I both modeled how to do so with our own lines. This time, the students became more animated and situated in the medieval world as they acted out and voiced their lines.

Kelsey expanded her "Drat my stew!" to "Drat, you dirty serf! You have wasted our precious salt, and that stew is now too salty for the king!" Maryann went from "Stitch up my boots!" to "Tailor! Can you not sew my tunic from your memory? Am I so much changed?" Throughout, the students attempted to take on the actions, demeanor, and language of the roles they played. When we had completed the montage, they broke into spontaneous applause. As we stepped back from the drama, the students commented on how well the montage brought to life what they had read about medieval castle life.

Through the remainder of the drama work the students *designed* other exhibits, *read* historical accounts, created more *artifacts*, were *interviewed* for public radio and television, planned a *marketing campaign*, read various accounts and legends of King Arthur, and created a *legend* about this castle. The students wanted to *consult* a real architect and a home restorer about the problems of restoration. One group of girls became interested with the notion of women warriors and read about Joan of Arc, Hippolyte and the Amazons, and an article about women in today's army. *Tableaux* or *frozen pictures* of medieval scenes were created physically and provided with captions. This led to drawings of *wall hangings* of events from the crusades to be used in one of the exhibit halls.

On the last day, the students created and enacted the events of a local legend about the visit and assassination of the king. This legend explained the demise of the castle. One student was familiar with Shakespeare's *Macbeth* and noted the connection. As possible museum *exhibits,* they created tableaux, which then came to life. These showed different possible ways in which the legend of the assassination might have happened.

The unit culminated with students *writing* verse in small groups. I suggested that the students retell part of the legend as it might have been told years later by minstrels at different courts. The students soon realized that different versions would develop. Then I asked how the legend might have changed over time and asked them to retell moments from the story again as if they were the grandchildren of the different minstrels. Again, change of content and shifting point of view became obvious. Finally, I asked if they would like to write what the minstrels might have sung and in groups they wrote verse to the melody of "Greensleeves," which they chose as appropriate. Each verse told the legend of the castle's fall but from a different point of view: the queen, her sister, her lady-in-waiting, the king's brother, the assassin, and the king's falcon, which had witnessed his death. After twenty minutes work, the students performed the song as if in the final exhibit for visitors touring the museum. Jeff's wife, Peggy, came to class that final day and delighted students and teachers by playing the lute and harp on her clavinova. The students sang to this evocative music as they played the parts of "minstrels" and "skops" telling tales of the castle a hundred years after it had fallen into ruins.

In this brief summary of the drama episodes used in this inquiry unit, we can see students' authentic engagement: asking questions and posing problems; seeking and finding information; reading and studying; considering, creating, and interpreting artifacts; wanting to interview community authorities; arguing, taking notes, telling stories, creating poems and songs; playing roles, discussing, and debating, connecting past and present, considering issues; analyzing and organizing information; representing and presenting what has been learned to others; considering and discussing ethical issues and much more.

We can also see Jeff and me as teachers authentically engaging with students and responding to their current questions and emerging understandings during the flow of carefully situated and purposeful learning. We attempted in various ways to continually raise the level of student learning: through our questions, our modeling, our cognitive and affective structuring of dramatic situations, our negotiations about dramatic action, and through reflection and feedback both within and outside the drama world. As teachers, we worked hard to build and frame dramatic situations and to guide students to perform their developing understandings through the use of different drama methodologies (mantle of the expert, scripted performance), various strategies (teacher in role, interviews, radio shows, rituals, narrative, choral montage, dramatic play, frozen pictures), and teaching techniques (questioning, pair work, small group work).

DRAMA'S ROLE IN AUTHENTIC TEACHING AND LEARNING

In the 1920s, John Dewey stressed that knowledge is the *means* rather than the end product of education yet, like many teachers, for years I assumed that education was individual "instruction" believing that students were learning if I gave them information or directed them to resources (Dewey 1922, 223). I had failed to cultivate what Heathcote calls "authenticity" in my classroom (4). As I watched the students in Maine become excited about life in a castle, memories flooded back about when I was a secondary school teacher of similar students in England years earlier. Although my students had read about feasts and jousts, and had themselves scrambled over actual castle ruins, after weeks of study they still seemed detached from the lives of medieval people. I had assigned work and graded it but I had done little of what I would now call teaching. I had not created contexts with students in which they could imagine the worlds of the books and explore their relationships with the societies, past, present, and future, which we talked about in class. I had done little either to assist students in the performance of their knowledge or to ensure that they would encounter alternative viewpoints that would challenge their thinking and provoke their creation of new understandings. Most significantly, I had regarded the interrelationships among students, subject matter, the world, and the teacher, as peripheral rather than central to learning—both theirs and mine.

Rethinking teaching, and learning to use drama for these new purposes, for me occurred gradually but simultaneously. The practices and philosophies of two renowned master teachers and theorists—Dorothy Heathcote and Cecily O'Neill—were seminal. Heathcote, with whom I studied for a year, uses the word "enabling" to capture the multifaceted stance of the authentic teacher who uses drama (Heathcote 1982, 1984). An enabling teacher works alongside students but is careful to choose when, and when not, to intervene so that at different moments she will allow, guide, shape, or challenge responses as students create and explore contexts and meanings together. Cecily O'Neill, who advised me during work on my doctoral dissertation, has stressed that drama, whether scripted or improvised, is "a place of disclosure . . . a way of seeing ourselves more clearly and allowing us to begin to correct whatever is amiss" (O'Neill 1995, 152). In working with her, I have recognized that the moves a teacher makes in drama are the selections and shapings of a dramatic artist; I have learned how to use theatrical structures that are available to the teacher in the improvised creation of powerful dramatic classroom experiences (O'Neill 1995). This book explores both the pedagogical and the artistic moves of Jeff and me as enabling teachers who strive for authenticity in the classroom.

For the past fourteen years, in my own elementary classroom and in all classrooms where I continue to teach as a guest, I have striven for authentic teaching and learning—in which connections are made among the lives of students and the histories, viewpoints, and cultures of people and places separated from the classroom by time or space.

As a teacher, I want to establish a laboratory atmosphere in which processes are learned as products are created, in which students' interests are harnessed and extended, and in which the knowledge and viewpoints of texts and people are explored and juxtaposed to foster growth of students' understandings. From the first time I visited Jeff's classroom, it was clear that authentic teaching and learning had become as important for him as they had for me. Later chapters in this book mostly revolve around examples from Jeff's classroom as we explore how drama can create the conditions for authenticity as it moves to the core of classroom teaching and learning. In this chapter I use the study and exploration of castles with the students in Maine to illustrate the integrative power of drama even when students are not in a supportive classroom context.

My problem—confusing instruction with education—was not unique. Tharp and Gallimore in their award-winning book *Rousing Minds to Life* (1988, 3–4) state it in the strongest possible terms: "In American classrooms, now and throughout the 20th century, teachers generally act as if students are supposed to learn on their own. Teachers are not taught to teach, and most often do not teach . . . All participants in the educational enterprise have shared an inadequate vision of schooling."

A remarkable consistency is emerging from various fields and educational policy camps about new criteria to assess the authenticity of classroom life. Many scholars and practitioners have come to embrace views of teaching which emphasize the *context* of learning; the *relationships* among teacher, students, and the world outside the classroom; as well as the significance of classroom *interactions*. Calls for "inquiry-based" education, "cooperative groupings," "caring communities," "holistic assessment," "integrated curricula," "learning as design," and "situated learning" are all examples of a shift from content-oriented and "drill-and-skill" views of education to more authentic meaning constructive approaches to classroom-based teaching and learning. The curriculum can no longer be regarded as a prepackaged thing which is delivered to students; curriculum is meanings which are *cocreated* by teachers and students in their day-to-day lives in the classroom. In drama, meanings about matters of significance are continually created as teachers and students imagine, interact, reflect, and inquire together in situated, integrated contexts.

Context of Learning

John Lounsbury pointedly argues that traditional education, despite a clear diagnosis, is ailing terribly: fragmented curricula, limited involvement and engagement of kids in planning and pursuing learning, the decontextualization of skills and concepts, the separation of school from the world, the imposition of higher standards without accompanying assistance in meeting those standards, ability grouping, the separation of educational programs (Lounsbury 1996). The real tragedy in this situation, as Lounsbury insists, is that there is widespread agreement regarding a solution, a solution that involves *proven* alternatives. Lounsbury's argument is echoed by that of James Beane in his influential *From Rhetoric to Reality*, by the brand new *Breaking Ranks* by the National Association of Secondary School Principals, and by progressive educators and educational researchers throughout the twentieth century (Beane 1993, Dewey 1938).

Researchers, theorists, and policy makers argue that the context of the classroom must create authentic *curriculum integration*. Both Lounsbury and Beane tell us separately that we must break down the artificial barriers of subject areas. Cognitive science also insists that language development, reading, writing, concept attainment and thinking in all knowledge domains "are profoundly inter-connected, and so *must be their instructional programs. . . . it is on that interface that the highest order of meaning is achieved, ensuring that tools of thought can be manipulated for the solution of practical problems in the experienced world.*" (Tharp and Gallimore 1993, 108). Further, the curriculum must become centered on problems and predicated on issues that are personally significant to students which will lead to greater concept acquisition, systematicity, applicability and extensibility of knowledge. Does this not sound like what happens in drama?

Within the Castle drama context, students asked their own questions, drove their learning onward, and proceeded easily to integrate knowledge from various domains to explore and search for solutions to the problems they had identified. For example, they combined using math to calculate the castle size to the science inherent in understanding moving granite blocks into place, to the historical and ethical issue of whether the castle should be reconstructed using only the tools and machines available in the Middle Ages. Further, in the context of the drama, Jeff and I frequently found ourselves touching on domains that crossed the boundaries of science, math, history, philosophy, psychology, sociology, and other disciplines.

Relationships Among Teachers, Students, and the World Outside Classrooms

Although the sixth graders in Maine constructed a rich system of conceptual knowledge about medieval castle life, their understandings were formed in a community of peers and teachers who collectively shared and shaped their views and insights. Over a complete year in his classroom, Jeff skillfully wove with his students what Nel Noddings calls a "caring community"—a space of deep trust where students felt safe in their explorations and analysis of relationships, roles, content, and their connections with the "real" world (Noddings 1992). However, after only a few hours in Maine, students' laughter, their readiness to cooperate, and especially their genuine but respectful disagreements signaled that such a community was beginning to develop.

An integrated curriculum focuses on the teaching and learning of transferable processes, strategies and skills—on knowing *how* much more than knowing *about* (what cognitive scientists call procedural rather than declarative knowledge). Such learning is inextricably part of relating classroom processes to the issues and concerns of the world outside the classroom. Factual knowledge wilts if not used; knowing how leads to further learning, and is integral to creating and finding meaning in life. John Dewey wrote that "the great waste of school is the child's inability to use what he knows in school; and to apply what he learns in school in his real life." (Dewey 1910).

Scholars have extended Dewey's insight to argue that students' understandings remain superficial unless their learning is grounded in rich, complex, multidisciplinary, "real world" *contexts*. In place of the prevalent decontextualized information-transmission mode of learning, education should become "situated" in authentic "communities of practice," which resemble professional or trade apprenticeships (Lave and Wenger, 1991). If students read, write, and think about content in ways similar to those experts whose jobs require them to read, write, and think, then students will similarly learn in much more complex and meaningful ways about, for example, critical reading, report writing—or history. Journalists, book editors, and archaeologists are among the professionals who initially learn key skills and processes as "apprentices." They learn in context and in relationship to content; they also learn by context-bound interactions and by indirect observation of more experienced teachers and peers as much as they learn by direct instruction.

Eliot Wigginton's *Foxfire* books demonstrated how students learn about themselves and about humanity when the stories and lives of local people outside the school building come inside the classroom to become the heart and soul of education. In a similar way, through collective imagination, teachers and students in drama connect with other times and places—real world issues from the past and from a distance come under the classroom microscope as they are recreated, experienced, savored, reinterpreted, and critiqued.

Drama in general, and the mantle of the expert approach in particular, *situates* learning in the professional relationships inherent in communities of expert practice. For example, in the Castle drama, it was the professional concern with history on the parts of the archaeologists and trustees of the National Trust that provided a context, and thus a reason and purpose, for the students' reading, writing, interactions, research, and evolving understandings.

Classroom Interactions

Over the years, as I recognized how experiences with drama intensified students' engagement in their exploration of themes and questions of personal interest, I also realized the unavoidably *interactive* nature of teaching and learning that makes the processes of education much more than either instruction or facilitation taken separately. As I discovered how effectively different views could be expressed, explored, and challenged in juxtaposition through drama, I began to recognize how teachers enable students to explore and extend their world views.

It also became clear to me from my classroom experiences that neither learning nor teaching are individual affairs. Learning is a product of social interactions; teaching is informed benevolent intervention that enables students to go beyond where they would on their own. Adult mediation is at the core of good teaching—a more competent adult who both participates and observes so that he or she can know when assistance is requested or may be needed by individuals and groups.

Few teachers confuse behavior with changes in meaning and most accept (often implicitly) Piaget's core concept that students must be given opportunities to construct their own understandings. For example, most elementary school teachers encourage experimentation with objects; in my secondary school classroom, I gave students time for library research and opportunities to redraft their writing.

Yet, "social constructivists" go further to argue that, as teachers, if we are unconcerned with the relationships and social interactions in classroom contexts then we ignore the core processes in which meaningful learning takes place. Students construct understandings as they talk, interact, and reflect on their experiences of the world *with* others—adults and peers (5).

Our notions of *how* students learn significantly affect *what* students learn. It causes me pain that I once implicitly accepted a mechanistic, behavioral view of learning, and thus concentrated on the acquisition of factual information students had to receive from others, especially me. My students learned information but my classroom work did not create self-motivated learners. Drama never became powerful for me until I constructed understandings *with* students.

But if you embrace the theory, as Jeff and I now do, that people socially construct understandings through joint productive activities, that in fact *all* complex meanings are actively and continually created with others, then you will begin to see both the importance and the tremendous power and potential of engaging students in dynamic interactions in imaginary situations. Using drama is a way for students to be motivated to use what they know, to learn new information for real purposes, and to create new understandings and theories of the world as they transform and apply this knowledge in new situations. In this way, drama guides students in learning how to learn, how to be aware, and how to be critical.

Grounded in the work of the Russian theorist Lev Vygotsky, social constructivists draw on his concept of the zone of proximal development (ZPD) to argue that teaching is an interactive process that builds on the competence of both teacher and student. The ZPD is "the distance between the actual developmental level determined by individual problem-solving and the level of potential development as determined through problem solving under adult guidance or in collaboration with more capable peers." (Vygotsky 1978, 86) In other words, teaching should happen in the ZPD, which lies between that which the students can grasp on their own and that which they can reach with the help of others. Tharp and Gallimore (p. 75) describe a powerful alternative to the "instructional" view of education when they emphasize the importance of teachers (and peers) "assisting" students as they "perform" their understandings. As Tharp and Gallimore put it: "teaching can be said to occur when assistance is offered at points in the ZPD at which performance requires assistance."

Tharp and Gallimore use the term "perform" as a metaphor for the ways in which meanings are created and shared with others—teacher and peers. The connections with the "performance" of drama are obvious. In classroom drama, as students interact they speak and enact their views and generate new understandings in the talk, writing, and art work that can permeate and surround their work. Meanings are elucidated when written texts are enacted in theatrical kinds of drama which "dramatize at the center of text" with scripts (e.g., story theatre, readers' theatre, and classroom theatre) as well as in the scriptless kinds of drama that "dramatize at the edges of texts" (e.g., story drama, narrative theatre, process drama) in which the process is the product (Wolf, Edmiston, and Enciso, 1997). A teacher assists performance both from the dramatic sidelines as a "side-coach" (Spolin 1963) in conferencing or facilitation, but also as a "teacher in role" (Heathcote 1984) who interacts with students as one of the fictional people in a drama world.

In this book, we are mostly concerned with the potential of scriptless *process* kinds of classroom drama, even though we also show the power of theatrical enactments of scripts that students wrote as a result of their inquiries. The students in Maine performed their prior and new understandings about the medieval world in and around the drama work that centered our week's work.

Teacher in Role

Although students will often agree to pretend that they are experts, interactions with the teacher *inside* the drama—using the strategy of *teacher in role*—are crucial in pressing for more depth in understanding. Heathcote pioneered this practice whereby the teacher structures the work from within the drama world by participating alongside the students.

The teacher who uses the strategy of a teacher in roles uses the medium of drama most effectively to enable learning. When the teacher, as well as the students, enters into the world of the drama he or she can speak from the position of any character in a story, any historical figure, or re-express any students' views in order to recontextualize, amplify, extend, or question ideas.

When teachers talk and respond in role, they place interactions firmly in a dramatic present so that participants must interact as if they are in the emerging drama world. Depending on our purposes, and the needs of the students, Jeff and I talked with the students as if we were also archaeologists, trustees, museum curators, or people who needed advice, information, or guidance. At various times alongside the students we became news reporters, marketing agents, and medieval castle servants.

Teacher in role provides a very efficient modality to shape the evolving drama world from the inside. Jeff and I monitored students' existing and developing understandings. Occasionally, we needed to correct an error directly that would have a significant effect in the drama world (e.g., one student thought that a medieval king could have had a gun to protect himself). However, usually we choose appropriate responses in role in order to guide students to more accurate or deeper understandings. In role, we could give instructions (as a museum curator, I demonstrated how to use a sword to dub a knight), provide information (as a trustee, Jeff gave geographical location and climate information as he talked with the students about the site), ask questions (as an archaeologist, I asked how they would care for the artifacts they found), and answer questions (as trustees, the students asked Jeff as an NPR news reporter why people in the United States were interested in English history). Further, in role we could indirectly provide details of historical and social contexts (as we talked about the proposed museum), demonstrate a professional stance towards events (as we "reminded" them of our previous work in successful museums), put students in an inquiring frame of mind (as we raised questions to see how they would respond), and provide a model of high expectations from which we could make students aware of their responsibility and the implications of their decisions. We also modeled how in addition to talk *in* the drama world, participants talk *about* the drama world—in order to clarify details, shift directions, make connections, and shape understandings.

Most important, working in role alongside the students raised both the status and stature of the students—they were continually treated with respect as knowledgeable, responsible people. Although Jeff and I shared information, ideas, and views with the students, we always genuinely supported them as they created their own understandings. In factual matters, however, students were *not* free to create whatever understandings they wanted. In thinking about concepts like "history," "justice," or "truth," we wanted students to connect their own life experiences with their experiences in the drama world and to forge new understandings as we interacted with them in the drama. As Heathcote has stressed: "The child . . . is discovering through the situation of [the drama]. Therefore he is not asking the teacher for the answer, he is offering the teacher a viewpoint and in return the teacher may offer another one" (Heathcote 1984, 85).

By interacting in role we were not just "pretending" to be interested in their ideas. We responded authentically as they both in and out of role shared their prior knowledge, the information they discovered, their genuine questions, and their developing interests. As the week progressed, they became more relaxed with each other and with us, more committed to the work, and more obsessed with the history of the castle.

CONCLUSION

During our last day of the Castle drama, small groups of students wrote stanzas for the ballad about the king's assassination that was sung to the tune of "Greensleeves." The context for writing was preparation for a possible exhibit near the end of the tour of the living history museum in the castle. The students had only twenty minutes to discuss and improvise, after which time the stanzas were put together and performed, to much laughter and delight.

The group decided to call their ballad "Queen Sleeve," and after hearing each other's, organized the stanzas in the following order.

Queen Sleeve (to the melody of "Greensleeves")

1–The Queen

One day the queen was counting
her money upstairs in her chambers.
She heard a cry from the throne below
And ran to find the King dying there.

"The will, the will!" he whispered to her.
"You must get it back, there are secrets there!"

But in his back there was a knife
That she knew to be from the king's brother's house.

2–The Assassin

I stabbed the king until he was dead
And with the will I then ran away
This will might save my people so
I held it so tight in my hand

If I could find the treasure,
My people could buy lots of bread.
But if I couldn't find it,
then no one would be fed.

3–The Lady in Waiting

The queen she heard a frightful scream
and ran to her beloved King.

I saw her face and heard her gasp as
she mournfully held her dying love.

The killer laughed an evil laugh
As he grabbed the will and burned the map.

The gallant knight arrived at last and killed
the fiend and that was that!

4–The Falcon

This is the tale of a bird of stealth
Who sees the crimes of the king with wealth
the king was slain for his evil deeds
For he killed and slayed for his greedy needs

(To the melody of the chorus of Greensleeves:)
Death, death to the innocent ones
Their wives, their daughters and even their sons

Death, death to the innocent ones
Their wives, their daughters, their hard-working sons.

5–The King's Brother

I loved the sister of the Queen
And loved the Kingdom of the King
But He feared me and the Love I bore
for the people, the serfs and the villeins.

So when he found I knew
of the treasure deep he had buried there
He threw me deep in his deepest cell
And left me so lonely to die there.

But love so true it would last past Death
Brought my own true love in the dark to me.
She sent my squire to the King for me
And my squire so true sought my vengeance!

6–The Queen's Sister, Woman Warrior

A warrior girl from the Queen's own blood
Led the knights and the people to justice.

So came the war and the castle fell
The people were fed; there's no more to tell.

She became the Queen and much was she loved
Just as she had loved the King's brother.

Each group sang their stanzas. Then as all of the students sang, they showed the action in *moving tableaux*—very short scenes in which they froze at the climax.

Preparing for the final performances enabled students to synthesize their understandings but provided yet another forum for revising views and making new connections. Meg and Kelsey, for instance, thought that if the assassin was the squire of the King's brother, then he would have had access to the king, which a serf would not. Robin suddenly felt that it needed to be clearer that the Queen's sister rose up against the king's ministers in order to lead the people to justice, much as Joan of Arc did—in response the last stanza was penned in a last minute frenzy.

As students shared their work they were both excited and suffused with feelings of accomplishment. Jeff and I too were excited, when in our final discussion with the students, their comments showed that they had achieved our aim of thinking about the constructed nature of history.

They were struck by the contradictory viewpoints in the ballad. Further, they realized that variant versions would have been received differently by different audiences and that some of these versions might not have survived over time. They regarded them as "facts," as much as any dates or details of artifacts.

Robin, in her role of trustee, said, "In our museum we don't know one single answer to everything, so we have many possible answers and show the lives of people from all their different eyes. . . ."

As an agent of the National Trust, I probed, "Can we ever really know the truth?"

Jessica answered, "Historians are all biased."

Kelsey explained, "Here we want to show the different biases, the different guesses about what and why things might have happened."

Meg added, "We never really know, we just think based on the little things we do know."

Robin concluded the discussion by stating, "The big thing I realized is that an event in history can be explained so many ways and from so many eyes."

Jessica's comments at the end of the work reminded us of the transformative power of drama: "I wish [teachers] would use [drama] more in schools because I don't like factoids. And schools don't give reasons to be interested. We would like school, or at least it would be bearable if it was like this. We've been learning factoids since first grade—we never learn what things are really like or why. People don't fill in the gaps—they just leave them there. Schoolbooks only put in the things that there's proof of—we don't learn why it's important or why kids should be interested in it."

When we use drama, we follow Jessica's advice—and Heathcote's—as we structure the work "to leave holes, very carefully, so that people fill them up with their own moment of discovery." (Heathcote 1982, 41) We use drama in our work to create relevant, challenging, productive, and authentic sites for student learning and discovery.

Whitehead (1962, 10) argued that "There is only one subject matter for education and that is Life in all its manifestations." Students often like drama because it is "fun" and teachers can justify using drama because it involves studying history or learning language. However, drama is most needed in schools because it expands the horizons of the classroom into the lives people live, have lived, and might live. Drama contextualizes content and ideas that students might otherwise consider arcane or removed from their world; through imagination and interaction with the teacher and other students drama connects the curriculum with students' own lives. As Jerome Bruner (1986, 128) stresses, "drama . . . is an invitation to reflection about the human condition."

NOTES

1. Dorothy Heathcote (1984) developed awareness of this crucial component of drama.

2. The significance of what I call the double consciousness of drama has been discussed by several scholars: Heathcote (1984), Bolton (1985), Boal (1979), O'Neill (1988), States (1985), and Edmiston (1995). Drama has a "liminal" nature because it exists on the boundary between the individual imagination and the external world. However, unlike other arts, process kinds of drama are made and experienced in the process of interactions among its creators. As a consequence, the world of the drama is both real and fictional; it is actually experienced by the students at the same time they know that they are constructing it. Heathcote describes the two stances of students as participants in the interactions of the drama and spectators on those interactions. O'Neill has noted the added spectator experience of students watching themselves. Bakhtin writes about the importance of understandings being "double voiced" or "dialogic." He analyzed in depth how the novel can be highly dialogic . Although Bakhtin did not regard theatre performances as very dialogic (largely because of the absence of an authorial voice on stage), the dramas we describe in this book are dialogic, espe-

cially when the teacher is actively involved. As teachers, we can shift the students' attention toward either their "single-voiced" experience or toward their "double-voiced" interpretation. We can assist students in their multifaceted ways of experiencing the world or we can assist in a critique of perspectives on the world.

3. This approach is described in detail in Heathcote and Bolton, 1995.

4. Heathcote (1984) has written a provocative and visionary article entitled "The Authentic Teacher and the Future," which is included in her collected writings.

5. Tharp and Gallimore, Wells and Chang-Wells (1992) are among the many social constructivists who have extended Vygotsky's original theories and insights.

2
Drama and Reading: Experiencing and Learning from Text

Jeffrey D. Wilhelm

In school, all you do is sit, sit, sit and write, write, write and get bored . . . you never get to do anything . . . I don't like school 'cause you can't do what you want. School blocks you from what you like to do.
— Libby, grade 7, beginning of school year

I really like learning with drama. I can get it because I'm doing and shaping things. Drama is like writing a story with your body . . . you get to learn things with all your feelings and all your body and by doing stuff with other people. And you have to listen to each other. It helps you a lot in knowing stuff.
— Libby, grade 7, end of school year

We accept the fact that the actor infuses his [sic] own voice, his own body, his own gestures—in short his own interpretation—into the words of the text. Is he not simply carrying to its ultimate manifestation what each of us as readers of the text must do?
— Rosenblatt, 1978, 13

THE WORK DRAMA DOES FOR READERS

I was teaching middle school reading and language arts when I first encountered *drama for learning*. During the same period, I was spending a lot of time feeling what my four-year-old daughter Jasmine calls "being FLUSTRATED!" I had 130 seventh-grade students, which included all of my school district's labeled population at that grade level. Any student whose file bore initials like LD (learning disabled), ED (emotionally disturbed), ESL (English as a Second Language), ADHD (Attention Deficit/Hyperactivity Disorder) had a seat in my classroom sometime during the day. Most of these kids and many others were reluctant, resistant, and sometimes even recalcitrant, readers. And going to school was not so much fun for any of us.

One of my journal entries put it this way: "I am FREAKING OUT and it is only the middle of September. Oh GOD, please don't let me start counting days already! 'Can't read!' 'Don't read!' 'Don't wanna read!' 'Don't know how to read!' Muttered swearing under their breaths. Simply refusing to work or do anything. Their comments and tortured behavior run through my brain at night. How am I going to help these kids to read and learn/to overcome their great towering RESISTANCE and frustrations? How am I going to help myself? How can I make them understand? I feel like a misunderstood dog in a Jack London story!" (September 1992)

During that same autumn, I was enrolled in Brian's graduate class on teaching with drama. But initially I was not seeing how drama could help me with my problem. I might be said to have been suffering from some resistance of my own. In another journal entry from the same month, I wrote: "Okay, this drama stuff is fun. It's enjoyable. But where's the SUBSTANCE? Where is the BEEF? I don't need a grab bag of neat little tricks. I can't afford to go with artsy-fartsy glitz-o-ramas. I need something to help me teach my kids how to read and how to learn because that is what they have no clue about. And if this or any other [graduate] class can't help me to do that than it is just a big . . . waste of time!" (September 1992).

Fortunately, Brian required us to use drama in our classrooms. And as I did, I slowly came to confront my own resistance. As I observed many of my more difficult students actually involving themselves in the drama activities, I felt relieved and happy. And when I began to see them help each other to read and to reflect on text in the context of our dramas, I became excited. And that is why I began to experiment and later to become such a proponent of using drama to teach reading and to support learning.

Throughout this book, Brian and I propose that drama can do powerful work of many different kinds for teachers and learners, and we illustrate this point with stories of students who have used drama in my classroom. In this chapter, I consider the particular kinds of work drama can do to support and extend the abilities of readers to (1) comprehend and experience what they are reading, and (2) to learn from, reflect on, and respond to text. In contrast to the extended Castle Drama described in Chapter 1, in which Brian created a single coherent and highly organic experience through a sequence of connected drama strategies, I explore the use of sometimes unconnected drama strategies that were designed to support students to make particular kinds of reading "moves" as they read different kinds of texts (Smith 1992).

Various studies have demonstrated that readers of stories must be able to enter the world of a story. (1) Drama can help readers to achieve that entry in different situations in which they may not know how or may have difficulty doing so. When drama is used for inquiry (*see* Chapter 5) or is used to structure the study of a theme (*see* Chapters 1 and 3) the teacher assists the students in the creation of a drama world that will frequently draw on multiple narratives and stories; the students are either framed with a fictional responsibility, for example as trustees or museum curators, or they regard themselves as researchers. However, when drama revolves around the reading of a story, the drama world *is* the story world. When students see themselves as readers who must transact with the text to construct meanings (a stance reluctant readers do not take, *see* Wilhelm 1997), this stance then frames a new and productive relationship with a text. Trouble arises when students see themselves as passive recipients of meaning and not as readers who produce significance. Drama can significantly affect students' perceptions of themselves as readers—for less proficient readers, drama can create some of the multilayered vivid experiences of texts that proficient readers already enjoy (Wilhelm 1997). Though certain drama methods (*e.g.,* mantle of the expert) can be highly effective at introducing a need for reading text and for enabling the sophisticated readings of specific texts (*see* Heathcote and Bolton 1995), I show here that individual drama strategies can also be used to assist students in gaining access to the world of a story, to support students as they struggle with written text, and to create meanings as the world of a story comes alive for them.

READING AND THE DRAMA WORLD: SIAMESE TWINS!

Many of my own students disliked reading and would do just about anything to avoid it. Other students did their best to improve themselves as readers, but struggled and floundered in dangerously deep waters as I merely shouted assignments and encouragement from a distant shoreline.

One such student was Libby, who had trouble comprehending text and trouble thinking about and applying what she had read. Libby became a case study student throughout a school year, and I use her story here to demonstrate the power of drama to assist students in becoming more attentive and competent readers. Libby's experience with drama is representative in many ways of other reluctant readers in my classes, even though she was more articulate than most about how and why drama was helpful to her. (To read about how drama supported highly resistant readers, *see* Wilhelm 1997.)

Like many teachers, I have considered and experimented for years with various techniques to actually teach and support my students in learning how to read, and also how to learn from and respond to text more powerfully. As a teacher-researcher during the past seven years, I have collected boxes of data and filled piles of notebooks with my observations as I attempted to document my emerging understandings of how students are best assisted to read and learn. These years of teacher research have led me to this conclusion: without a doubt, drama is one of the most powerful discoveries and techniques at a teacher's disposal for helping students to become more masterful readers and learners.

As educators, we all know how important good reading skills are to our students. I have always regarded reading of any kind, but especially of literature, as a unique and powerful way of knowing our deepest human concerns, and of knowing our personal and social possibilities. Reading is also the foundation of school success and is the basis of most cognitive development and thought in our culture. Tharp and Gallimore (1988, 109) argue that "[t]his enterprise—the school-based instruction in comprehension of written text—is indeed the main route toward establishing societal systems of discourse meanings that create both the intermental and intramental capacities for verbal thinking." In other words, reading comprehension is the foundation for the abilities to think with others and on one's own by using verbal symbols. Or to put it even more clearly: if students don't learn to read well they will be severely handicapped both in school and in life.

Many national reports and assessments have confirmed what cognitive scientists have long argued—that reading is a foundational cognitive competency that many students lack. Many students in the United States do not truly "read" because they do not understand the connection between text, made up of abstract verbal symbols called words, with everyday objects, concepts and systems (*see* the National Assessments of Educational Progress 1981 *ff.*). How to address this situation is something I have struggled with throughout my career, as when I mused in my journal that

"I don't really teach kids how to read. I assign, I spout facts, I share my interpretations and I grade. But what am I doing to actually help the kids read? I know how to teach writing. But how do you teach reading? It's like good reading is some giant magical mystery tour and some kids are missing it—they are not connecting—they are out of the loop! And so am I!" (April 1988).

Wood (1980, 290) writes that effective instruction in reading "involves a continuous integration of language and action" and of explicitly making the connection between the concrete world of reality and the abstract words on the page. This simple lesson is one that I did not use in my teaching and is one that many reluctant readers have never learned. This, in turn, can explain their poor comprehension and their reluctance. And although I did not know it yet, it is a lesson that dramatizing text powerfully teaches. Abstract thought, write Tharp and Gallimore "require[s] a continual freshening by example and a testing against sensory data" (p. 110). Drama is a cognitive tool that concretizes the abstract, making it sensory and available.

Drama creates a virtual world—or mental model—from the textual symbols called words. This, as will be seen later in this book, is essential not only to reading, but to mathematic and scientific understanding.

But how is this virtual world created? Being interested in what expert readers do and how I could encourage my less able readers to do the same thing, I turned to the field of literary theory and read widely there. I found that Louise Rosenblatt (1978) asserts that the abstract text acts both as a stimulus that activates the reader's past experience and as a guide for selecting, transforming, and ordering that past so that it is integrated with the text into a new experience.

Rosenblatt and others have emphasized that reading research and instruction focus almost exclusively on how a reader interprets, evaluates, and reflects on the evoked world of the text. (This pretty much summed up my own teaching practices!) Even so, little attention has been paid to the prerequisite creation of a story world (or mental model) by a participant reader. Students are nearly always asked to interpret readings they have not been helped to experience. And without participation, the reader has no experience and no learning to reflect upon. Is it any wonder that so many are unsuccessful? (2)

But what does a reader actually have to *do* to be successful? (3) In my own teaching, I was sure that many reluctant readers did not know how to, or even know that they should, participate in entering and creating a "story world" (or a mental model, in the case of expository text) of what they read. Certainly schooling has focused on decoding text instead of reading for experience and for meaning (Gambrell and Heathington 1981); little if anything has been done to help students to read in an engaged experiential fashion that allows for powerful connections and applications to be made between text and life. In fact, the typical recitation, questioning, and discussion patterns in schools in the United States have served to reinforce unengaged readers' passivity and their attitude that meaning is to be received from the text instead of constructed with it (Johnston & Winograd 1983).

My reading and subsequent teacher-research demonstrated that unengaged and reluctant readers do not go beyond the text and they do not actively create meaning as they elaborate on the text (Enciso 1990; Thomson 1987; Wilhelm 1992, 1997).

I came to conclude that this lack of involvement and participation on the part of less expert readers explains their negative reading attitudes and achievement (Wilhelm 1997). It also explains why they fail to take on the many stances and moves of expert readers. As Enciso's work was the first to show me, more expert readers not only enter into textual worlds, but they also intensely visualize settings, characters, and situations, take on various roles and positions inside this world, connect their lives to their reading, complete the world by inferring and filling gaps, and engage in a variety of activities to reflect on the meanings they have constructed with the text (Enciso 1990, 1992, 1994; Wilhelm 1997). This also makes a case for why a highly participatory and natural language event like drama can be used with reading to help reluctant students take on the stances and moves of more engaged readers.

In drama, the imaginative cocreation of the story world is made visible. Students can work together to create meaning, and then step outside the drama world to monitor how, why, and how well they did so. When drama is used for the actual reading of the text of a story, then the drama world must parallel the story world or else the drama will not support the reading of this particular text. And even though students and teachers work together to support a rich, imaginative, and valid reading through their drama, the experience is always also intensely individual—because students will have explored their own particular part of the drama world by bringing their own particular experiences to bear—which is exactly what expert and highly engaged readers have been shown to do.

Certainly, less proficient readers must learn to think differently about the reading act by learning what to do and how to participate in the construction of meaning. Drama can provide the necessary assistance by helping novices to see and to do the things expert "reading participants" do to evoke and experience text (4).

As I struggled to understand how to teach reading through several ongoing studies with students, I found that "seeing" what is read is a key to comprehension (Wilhelm 1995, 1997). Purcell-Gates (1991) likewise found that less-proficient readers were at a loss for strategies for stepping into and sustaining "envisionments." They did not make use of strategies for creating meaning by building relationships with characters, taking their perspectives, and imagining, visualizing, and manipulating secondary worlds. Gambrell and Bales (1986) found that students did not "spontaneously employ mental imagery as a strategy" and would not do so after being assigned or directed to. And if students do not "see" what they read, then they have not had an experience with text that they can savor, think about, or use.

This kind of "seeing" and concrete realization of textual meanings depends on the use of information "outside the text" (such as personal experience) and the use of information from "inside the textual experience" (such as a sense of the rules, parameters, and development of the experience). All these components are necessary to both learning and to the creation and sustaining of what Brian calls "a drama world" (Edmiston, 1991). Again, we can see why drama is a potent device for helping students to bring their background experiences, schema knowledge, interests, desires, and questions to bear on the reading of text—and for visualizing and realizing rich mental models by expressing the knowledge that is made available from their reading transaction (5).

Rosenblatt (1978) forcefully asserts that "the benefits of literature can emerge only from creative activity on the part of the reader himself" (p. 276). Readers must learn to actively participate in constructing meanings as they fill in the forms outlined by written cues. Eco (1978) goes so far as to describe reading as the taking of "inferential walks"; he says that texts provide the reader with *point a* and *point e* and require that the reader fills in appropriate *points b, c, and d* from his or her own prior experiences as a person and a reader.

Along these same lines, Hansen (1981) and Langer (1984) have found that encouraging readers to actively involve themselves in creating and filling in these kinds of meanings—such as that required by the creation of drama and visual art in response to reading—in itself creates a context for more sophisticated comprehension, more highly elaborated meanings, and more easily made connections between what is known and what is coming-to-be-known. This is because background schemata are necessarily activated and built on, which is a foundational aspect of proficient reading. Active, participatory experiences are known to increase motivation and concept attainment in learning across knowledge domains (Bransford 1979; Reid 1988).

In fact, research from such various fields as literary theory, language development, educational psychology, artificial intelligence, and cognition demonstrates that reading is the active construction of meaning and supports the notion that the use of dramatic activity would help readers experience and learn from texts (6).

Luckily, at the point at which I was first coming to understand the very active and participatory nature of reading, Brian was there to help me begin using drama to support my floundering readers.

LIBBY LEARNS THROUGH DRAMA

As I began to use drama for this purpose of modeling and supporting the strategies and moves of active readers, I first tried a variety of techniques *as* students read a shared class novel. Later, I describe strategies that were used to help students after reading to reflect on their reading experience. Drama is very effective before reading because students are helped by it to become interested in the text, to activate or build pertinent background knowledge, to make predictions, and to prepare to read. During reading, drama can be used to support the active creation of meaning. After reading, drama can be used to reflect and think along the edges of the text, and to go beyond the text to explore further textual and personal possibilities.

One especially effective drama strategy that I have used has been what I have come to call the *carousel* or *revolving role play*. (This idea was first introduced to me at a conference presentation by Cecily O'Neill.) With this strategy, students initially each take on a single role (often characters, but sometimes mathematical concepts, scientific principles, objects or other ideas; *see* Chapter 6) from a text and pair up with another student playing another role. They are given a topic to discuss or a task to complete in a short one to two minute role play. Each role-play topic or situation parallels one from the reading. Through a series of role-plays, students take on various roles and often revisit and replay previous roles.

For instance, during our reading of *The Incredible Journey* the students imagined that they were lost in the wilderness (just like the animal characters in the book). Half the class would all play the role of a person who has had some limited success hunting and fishing, and though hungry, still has some food (this parallels that of Tao the cat). The other half of the class adopts the role of a person who has no food and is beginning to starve (paralleling the role of Bodger the terrier). Each successful hunter would match up with one person who is starving. During their role play, the hungry character begins by asking for food. A short role-play ensues during which each pair of students must explore how this problem of survival is to be worked out between them. After the role play, students would report on their discussions, dilemmas, and feelings.

Each hunter would then become a friend and advocate for the starving person (paralleling the role of Luath the Labrador) as roles are changed. The starving person becomes the successful hunter. The friend thinks people on this journey will starve unless some way to share food is worked out. Each person finds a new partner playing the other role. A new role play begins as the two role players try to work out such an arrangement.

After completing each role play in such a drama, the students take on a new role, find a new partner, and take on a new task. This can continue indefinitely. Quite often, I use the revolving role plays for eight to ten minutes at the beginning of class to refresh students' memories of yesterday's reading and to activate their imaginations and schematic knowledge to prepare them for what they will read today. Over the course of several days, students will play all major roles from a story and adopt each role several times. I used the carousel strategy described here for as long as it took the class to read the novels, *The Incredible Journey* and *Roll of Thunder, Hear My Cry,* about two weeks in all for each book. I used the carousel strategy daily during the reading of these books and each student usually took on anywhere from eight to twelve different roles, and usually had the opportunity to play each major role three or four times.

Although students were required to work with a completely new partner after each role play on any given day, quite often students made sure they paired up with a favorite partner once each day. Sometimes, these pairs continued to use drama strategies on their own as they read and explored the meaning of the required text or of other texts like "free-reading" books. In some of these cases, clearly a kind of peer assistance and peer tutoring was going on, with the students supporting each others' reading and experience of the story. One such case was the pair of Janne and Libby.

Janne was a highly engaged reader who read constantly. She was a short girl with long blonde hair and a perky personality. She was a big fan of equestrian sports and of country music, particularly the Gatlin brothers. She often seemed to prefer the company and conversation of adults to that of her classmates. In class, she was usually fairly reserved. Drama was one of the few situations in which she would openly share her thoughts and feelings with the class.

Janne paired up quite early in the year with Libby, and they made sure they worked together on various projects, and always worked together during drama. Libby was a very slight girl with long brown hair and watery blue eyes, and usually wore T-shirts and jeans to class. She shared Janne's love of horses and eventually her love of drama. Libby, like many of my students, was labeled as LD (learning disabled) and was considered to have a comprehension problem. Libby told me, "I like reading"; she was often seen carrying a book. However, she certainly struggled with the reading process, had difficulty answering simple comprehension questions, and a terrible time answering inferential questions. She indicated that she was not a good reader because she "flunked quizzes . . . I sometimes don't know what the questions are even talking about." On an Analytical Reading Inventory (Woods and Moe 1980) administered at the beginning of the year, Libby's word recognition was nearly at grade level (Grade 6), and she was able to answer literal comprehension questions up to this grade level. However, she was unable to answer inferential or evaluative questions for selections beyond the Grade 2 level.

She particularly enjoyed "stories about girls like me" and voiced a rabid dislike for the "reading they make you do in school." She liked books "when I get to choose" and she usually chose series books like the American Girls, Baby-sitters Club, or Nancy Drew for her free-reading choices. She indicated that she ran into difficulty when she didn't recognize settings, situations, or characters as being familiar. "I have trouble where the characters aren't like me or when I can't compare things in the story to stuff that I know about." This was very frustrating to her, and her eyes would sometimes appear to fill with tears when experiencing difficulty with comprehension.

What she described was no great surprise, because it is clear that difficulties with comprehension usually are bound up in a lack of necessary background information or the inability to access and activate the necessary background "schema" or knowledge structures. Libby had a very flat response even to stories that she said she liked, discussing them as if they were reports, or links of facts. "First Nancy went to the ski hut with her friends. Then one of her friends disappeared. Nancy asked what happened." She did not describe visual experiences, relationships with characters, taking on perspectives or experiencing feelings as she read, even though she was actively encouraged to do so.

When reading a story in class that was less familiar to her than the stock characters and situations of the few genre series she liked, Libby would struggle and was unable to answer questions about character, setting, and situation. "It's really hard to tell," she'd report, "the book really doesn't say much about how things are." She had little memory of scenes she had just read, and seemed to have little available prior experience to hook and connect new reading experiences to—especially if characters were too dissimilar to Janne and her sister, and the situations too unlike those of her own life or her genre fiction. She often critiqued the stories we read in class as "kind of plain." She once explained that "It's the characters. I don't feel like they're like me. I don't get the story. It's just kind of plain. Nothing is happening. I don't feel like I know anybody so I don't like it very much."

She seemed at a great loss to enter into and engage with unfamiliar kinds of material. Reading was better for her, she told me, "when I don't work so hard on the words because I already know stuff about the people and places," which statement again emphasizes the importance of activating prior knowledge and applying it to one's reading. As noted, even when she literally comprehended the text, she did not enter into the world or create mental models that described and informed new understandings. Her reading was tied to textual detail, while she was failing to build on these details to elaborate textual suggestions or possibilities. For Libby, because enjoyable reading was about "something you already know about," the power of reading to provide new experiences and understandings was denied her. Libby saw reading as cracking the code of letters to identify words (which was something she could do), but not as something that required the application of her own experiences to the creating of a new and unique experience.

Drama is helpful in this regard, as David Booth tells us (1990) because "drama encourages children not to be satisfied with immediate, simplistic solutions but to keep exploring, peeling away the layers that cloud the meaning, it can help develop the 'what if' element that must be brought to print if true reading is to occur" (p. 193).(8)

In my analysis of adolescent reading expertise (Wilhelm 1997), I found that highly engaged readers used a variety of strategies to *achieve entry* into story worlds; to *enliven the story world* by relating to characters and seeing characters, settings and situations; to *connect to and complete the story world* by making explicit personal connections, and by inference and elaboration; and to *consider the text* by reflecting on its significance, the construction of the text, the reader's personal transaction with the text, and on the nature of the author and reader as expressed through the transaction.

In Libby's case, she could enter a familiar story in genre fiction and enliven that world in very limited ways. She did not have a repertoire of strategies at her disposal for use with texts outside this limited scope, and she never made moves to connect to, complete, or consider the text. When we began to use drama during the second quarter of the school year, the dramas helped her to begin using these kinds of strategies, first by providing external and socially supported models for these moves and later through

Libby's internalized model of reading as the creation of a "drama world," which she used on her own to mobilize various strategies for making these kinds of moves.

Brian argues that as readers we must go "inside" a book to adopt perspectives, become characters, empathize with them, and critique their actions. He points out, however, that little is done in classrooms to help students get into this mindset. When we talk about readings or answer questions about it, we are always outside the world of the story and no longer experiencing it. In drama, however, our private "story worlds" merge with those of others into a shared drama world in which we can walk around and interact with other people in role (Edmiston 1993). In drama, as in engaged reading, we are aware on one level that we are reading or dramatizing, but on another, we are very much immersed in the middle of events that concern us or are happening to us. Heathcote (1984) tells us that we are deeply affected by drama action because we feel its reality, which occurs in what she terms *now and imminent time.* Cognitive psychology (Conant, Budoff and Hecht 1983; Vygotsky 1962) has also noted the intense seriousness with which children enter into and experience game-like and dramatic situations.

Like so many other students, Libby indicated great difficulty in achieving this entry with her reading. After reading Chapter 1 of *The Incredible Journey,* Libby reported that "it's kind of confusing. I don't really get it." She could neither name the major characters, identify their situation, describe the surroundings in which the action took place, or make predictions.

While reading Chapter 2, I monitored the students' comprehension, and intervened with drama work whenever understanding seemed to break down. For example, there was this passage on page 21:

> Twenty minutes passed and no move was made; then suddenly the young dog rose, stretched himself, and stood looking intently down the drive. He remained like this for several minutes, while the cat watched closely, one leg still pointing upwards; then slowly the Labrador walked down the driveway and stood at the curve, looking back as though inviting the others to come. The old dog rose too, now, somewhat stiffly, and followed. Together they turned the corner, out of sight.

When asked to summarize this passage, Libby could not. I decided to use what I call an *analogy strategy* in which I would ask students to enact a personal experience that paralleled in some way a scene from the reading. Here I asked groups of three students to *mime* hanging out with their friends during the summer. One of the three would try to convince the others to join her in some kind of activity while the other two resisted. In Libby's group, Libby herself mimed heading to the local diamond to play softball while her two classmates yawned and ignored her. She finally convinced them to join her after miming the eating of a snack after the game. Upon rereading the scene, Libby immediately saw the connection: "the big dog is like me—he's trying to convince them to go!"

This and several other scenes from the chapter were acted out briefly and frozen at their climax into a *frozen picture* (also known as a *tableau*). For some of these, I asked the students to provide a caption; for others, I tapped students in the frozen picture, at which point they came alive to report on their feelings and motivation, to explain what they were doing, or to answer questions. At the end of class, I asked one group to quickly run through all of their frozen pictures to provide us with a *slide show* of major scenes from the chapter. Libby's group glided from action to frozen picture and caption to action again in a subtle flow from story participation to story spectating.

After her work during this class period, Libby was unusually effusive. "It was so cool. I could kind of see and feel what was happening." In the first scene, "it was like the dog saying, 'Let's be adventurous, let's do something!' and when he was saying that, it was like I was saying it too and I could feel how much he wanted to do it." Later she told me, "it was like I was watching the story happen like a video and I could feel what was happening really good . . . it was exciting!" She continued on to recount several life situations that paralleled those in the book. Libby's energy level was impressive because she was usually very reticent in class. Clearly, the dramatic reenactments had made the "secondary world" accessible to Libby and with that world various meanings came alive.

Before reading Chapter 3, I asked the students to engage in some *guided imagery* and *dramatic play*. In guided imagery, students were asked to imagine scenes in their minds—and sometimes to draw them—as I read descriptions from the book, elaborated on these descriptions, and sometimes played music with an appropriate mood. On this day, I asked the students to imagine they were in the woods, read some descriptions from the book, and added some details. The students drew on paper that which they had seen in their minds. Libby's picture was all black and green, a dark picture with towering pines and very small animals huddled on the dark ground. "As I drew the picture, I kind of felt like it was scary . . . I don't know why . . . but that's what I think it looks like." Again, she said, "this is so cool, to kind of see what the things in the book look like!"

During *the dramatic play,* students were given a prompt or situation to be used as a stimulus for imagining or filling out a story event. In this case, I asked the students to role play an imagined discussion between the animals after that first night—how would they feel? What would they want to do? In her scene, in her role as the old dog Bodger, Libby indicated that she "wanted to go home. I'm tired and I'm hungry and I'm scared. I just don't know what we've gotten ourselves into!" (Libby later revised this interpretation as she came to the conclusion that Bodger might be hungry and tired, but never scared. I'm guessing that the drama work helped her to understand and become sensitive to Bodger's character in a new way and therefore to later revise her interpretations of his experience.)

After this short episode, students were asked to write a *diary entry* in role. Libby wrote: "It's pretty dark under all the pine trees and so we slept pretty late we were so tired. I think we need to find the old road again . . . maybe even go home where there's food."

Here Libby is entering into character, visualizing settings and making personal connections between her life and the text to sustain a secondary world and play with meanings in that world by making inferences and seeing possibilities. She told me that the drama "reminded me of being in the woods. . . When I read best, I guess I feel like I'm in a drama. I make up surroundings and make up scenes. I understand it better." Libby was the only one of several students I studied who regularly made the connection between drama and reading. A bit later she advised me that "Writing and reading are easier if you are a character. It's harder to write if you're not somebody. You should let us do more of that." Libby points out here that in drama you have to be somebody and take a perspective. This perspective-taking aids reading and writing, both of which are generative, meaning-constructing activities.

We continued to use revolving role play throughout our reading of the book. In Libby's class, we focused mostly on becoming characters and enacting scenes from the story—mostly actual scenes, but often scenes that we called *missing scenes* that we felt were implied by the story or could have happened. In this way, I was trying to raise my expectations for the students and push them to imagine not only the text, but what might happen beyond the literal text. We also made use of the *correspondence strategy* in which students wrote and responded in role to diaries, postcards, letters, news flashes and advertisements.

During a *To Tell the Truth* game after our reading, I asked various students to play at *hotseating*. In hotseating, a student plays the role of a character and answers questions as if at a press conference. We also played *inner hotseating* by having another student, standing behind the character, respond as the inner self of the character might. In other words, we acted a like the characters in Woody Allen's *Annie Hall,* presenting ourselves to the world in one way, at the same time the subtitles—revealed in our game by the inner self—tell what we're really thinking, feeling, and wanting to say.

During our game, Libby wrote down several questions for Tao, all of which were inference questions regarding Tao's feelings and motivations during different times in the story. "Why did you fight the MacKenzies' cats and how did you feel about it?" "How did you feel about Helvi and do you miss her?" "How would you have felt if Bodger died and were you ever worried about this?"

When she played the role of Bodger, she elaborated at length on her in-role feelings in approaching home, hearing Luath the Labrador bark with joy while he, Bodger, still limped along the trail, and the great joy she felt at being reunited with her master, Peter. When her alter ego said that he felt joy, but also relief, at finally reaching home, Libby nodded, and said, "What I really want is a big bowl of dog food!" To her alter ego's response that he had worried about making it home, Libby disagreed during our reflection time. "I think after the first few days he knew he was going to make it. He wasn't going to let himself not make it." At this time she launched into one of her longest sharings of the year, about her experience with horses and their great fortitude during equestrian events.

When I observed that all of Libby's questions and responses had to do with feelings that weren't actually reported in the actual text, she told me that "I think reading is really about feelings, about seeing and feeling things . . . That's what I like about the drama, in a regular class you can't share your feelings."

This was a real change for Libby, who had indicated through earlier summaries and responses that she thought reading was simply decoding word-level meanings and identifying ideas or events.

Whenever they had the opportunity, Libby would work with her friend Janne. Janne seemed to invite Libby into the drama world and helped her to do particular kinds of things inside that world. When I interviewed the girls about what was happening between them in this clear case of "peer assistance," Libby said "Janne helps me to become a character and to figure out how they are going to act, then I can go on from there." When I pursued her thinking about how Janne helped, Janne said that "In the drama, I try to do what she does. I don't call her by her name but by the character's name. She asks me questions and I try to answer them. She listens to me . . . I ask her to . . . I allow her to express her thoughts and feelings. I try to make her feel happy if she's sad and I react the way I should. Maybe she'll help me to solve problems, maybe say 'What do you think we should do?' or 'Remember when you did such and such?'"

What is interesting about this is that though Janne is clearly the expert reader, Libby helps Janne to help her, and in fact works to help create and sustain the drama world. Janne provides only the assistance necessary for Libby to take on as much responsibility as possible for enlivening the reading through drama. This scaffolding, or assistance, takes the forms of modeling, questioning, explaining, and prompting. Libby also assists Janne in considering new ideas and other perspectives. The drama work helped Libby to see that she and Janne were experts in different ways. In the previous chapter, Brian highlighted Bakhtin's idea of the need for multiple viewpoints to achieve complex understandings. Libby expressed to me that she provided new viewpoints as she added "questions" and "sometimes more feelings" to her drama work with Janne, and that she helped Janne to "see more stuff"—particularly from the perspective of other characters Janne considered to be less important than the major characters whose roles she seemed to assume as she read.

Libby told me during a different interview that during her reading of *The Incredible Journey* she "felt like Tao [the cat] . . . quiet, shy, can do stuff for myself even though people think I need help. OK on my own but I like to be around my friends." At the beginning of the book, Libby said she had "trouble understanding what was going on . . . trouble understanding the characters . . . but now I can see the animals are just like people." Asked how she had come to this realization, she explained "By being them with my body. I got to do things and make decisions and things with my body when I was imagining I was them so I felt like them . . . and that's just how it felt in my body."

For Libby, using her body was an important part of learning through drama. For other students it was making visual representations through drawings, creating postcards, or making frozen pictures or tableaux in person or on paper. One of the most supportive things about drama is that it combines different kinds of concrete signs with the abstract nature of text: students create the meaning of the text through their words—both written or spoken, kinesthetically through the motion and positioning of their bodies, visually through their stance, artwork, and observation of others; emotionally through their feelings, often expressed in gesture, music, or writing; intrapersonally as they reflect and interpersonally as they create shared meanings by reacting and responding to the dramatic actions of others. Drama incorporates various sign systems and all the multiple intelligences identified by Gardner (1983) at one time. The work of many teachers, though I am thinking particularly of Gallas (1994) in her description of "bad boys," has shown how kinesthetic learning is very valuable in promoting better behavior and more competent learning for many students who have difficulty with classrooms run in a traditional basis.

DRAMA AND EXPERT ASSISTANCE

Because of its social nature, teaching through drama makes use of a central Vygotskian insight *that learning proceeds from the group to the individual.*

Cognitive science has clearly demonstrated that children acquire their first language instruction through interaction with more competent speakers (Bruner 1983; Spiedel 1987; Vygotsky 1962). That we learn socially through purposeful interactions with others who are more expert than we are is also true for later vocabulary development, reading, and other discourse competences. Signs and symbols take on their shared meanings as they are used through "joint productive activity" (Tharp and Gallimore 1988). Through interaction, "intersubjectivity" is achieved and the students' abilities are stretched. Intersubjectivity means that the child, student, and less expert peer have come to share the more sophisticated understanding of their caregiver, teacher, or more expert peer because of and through their interaction. Intersubjectivity, as in the case of Janne and Libby, means that they now share and can use this higher-level meaning because they have come to mutually integrate their cognition in the context of task performance.

During this process, the "expert" first takes on the responsibility for providing whatever support is necessary to the satisfactory completion of the task at hand. As the "learners" master the necessary skills, we see a steadily declining level in the "expert's" responsibility for task performance and an increase in the learner's responsibility. This is Bruner's fundamental "handover principle"—the child who was a spectator is now a participant (Bruner 1983, 60). The developmental task of the learner of any new skill is to move from being regulated by another to being regulated by the self. "Outer speech" between the expert and learner becomes "inner speech" as the learner internalizes the "intersubjective discourse" and uses this shared way of making meaning to come to think for herself (Vygotsky 1962). Again, in the drama Janne was usually the expert, but this role was sometimes played by Libby. The drama work allowed both girls to continually play both roles.

(Although we have focused on the relationship between Janne and Libby during their use of various drama strategies, all of this activity took place in a wider context of drama activity that involved the whole class and me as the teacher-in-role. We were continually able to support, extend, and provide a safety net for each other.)

This transfer from external to internal thought is socially supported and interpsychological because before becoming entirely independent, the learner uses language to operate on her own with the safety net of the observing peer or adult, and adopts the language and understanding they have shared to ask for assistance. For example, in his analysis of joint puzzle solving, Wertsch (1979, 19) found that the learner begins to ask for strategic directions, for instance, "What part do I do next?" before completely internalizing all strategy use on her own.

This is why reading must be made "visible" or "external" and supported in social use through oral reading, lap reading, bookmaking, story illustration, dramatization, and the like for reading competence to be achieved. We simply cannot expect students to learn new competences by being told what to do or by being asked to respond to questions. It has been made compellingly clear that readers need the inner workings of other readers to be made visible. Novices always need social support in the context of joint productive activity to achieve new understandings and master new skills (Tharp and Gallimore 1988) (8).

Drama can work in this way as an external representation of the internal state of the more expert reader. Externalizing the interior world of the reader allows the teacher to bring the text into a closer relationship with the students and makes engaged reading more accessible to them.

THE MANY TEACHERS IN A DRAMA

Drama provides an opportunity for multiple "teachers" to educate each other about how to read experientially and how to reflect in various ways on that reading. This was the case as I helped to complicate and expand the drama as the teacher-in-role, as other students fleshed out the drama, and as pairs like Janne and Libby worked with each other. Drama, when used as described here, also helps participants to help each other in building a repertoire of meaning-making strategies; this kind of repertoire building is largely ignored by the information-driven focus of traditional schooling.

First, the students using drama learn that they need to bring their own thoughts into an interaction with those of the *author*, who is attempting to assist them into a new experience and new understandings. Janne constantly modeled for Libby the attention she paid to the author and the text and helped her to be helped by the author's text. Likewise, the *teacher* must constantly help the students to go back and forth between the author's words and their response to them. This was something I did both in and out of role as we reflected each day on our drama work, its value, credibility, and consistency with the text we were studying. *Students* must learn that to translate print into meaning, they must first crack the code of print and must then apply their own experiences to that broken code to flesh it out into a virtual reality. Drama work makes this process visible. Finally, *groups* can test and clarify the implication of the text collectively, so that each person can see the differences among various interpretations, share stances and strategies, and make decisions about one's own response (Booth 1990; Fines and Verrier 1974; Moffett and Wagner 1984; Wagner 1976).

In drama, students are helped to move from their experience to the text and to build a relationship between the two that is woven into a relationship and a response. This weaving of past and present understandings is at the core of what we call *authentic* learning (*see* Chapter 1) in which the learning is personally relevant and connected to student lives, is socially significant, and can inform and be used in the future living experiences. Past experiences must be connected to current text to complete that experience. Only when that happens can a new response emanate from the relationship of experience and text through reflection on the reading.

This new and larger structure of understanding is formed from an exchange of meaning that has both intramental and intermental planes. It is essential that the new learning must be reconciled with past learning. We know that *authentic* learning is patterned and systematic and extensible— able to be built on and applied in new situations. Likewise, we know that less able readers' beliefs about knowledge keep them from supposing that consistent interpretations across events are possible or desirable. Unengaged and less proficient readers regard knowledge as a basket of unrelated facts (Anderson 1984).

In drama, thought is made visible and is related to past and future. Dramatic thought and new understandings can be constructed, manipulated, supported, and guided through assistance from the author, from the context and structure of the text and the drama, from the teacher operating both inside and outside the drama, from peers mutually participating together, and finally from self-tutoring. This is a core goal of authentic teaching and learning—to reach the point at which the self can stretch and thus teach the self. This process is not achieved, however, without considerable support and caring social relationships. As teachers, we can be significant in creating the conditions in which such critical support occurs both with and among our students. It is important to note that none of the kinds of learning trials, the mutual sharing to develop new strategies, nor instructional conversations that occur in the context of drama work require an overhaul of curriculum or of schools, but only of how we define teaching and learning.

DRAMA ON THEIR OWN

Later that year, we proceeded to use drama to explore implications of the text, of using reading as a springboard to explore understandings suggested by the text, and by presenting these to others. As we pursued this more reflective purpose, Janne and Libby read Lurlene MacDaniel's *Somewhere Between Life and Death* together for the purpose of creating a joint *dress-up book report*. The story, according to the girls' summary, involves two sisters, Erin and Amy. Erin is older than Amy by sixteen months and must, according to Janne, "learn how to say goodbye to her little sister."

Originally, Janne was running the show and planned that the two girls would do the scene where "Amy turns towards death."

> I thought dramatizing one scene could capture the whole meaning of the book. In this scene Amy turns towards death and Erin has to accept that she will die. I told Libby that if we could do that scene, I knew we'd show people how Amy was trapped in a world between life and death . . . She and Erin fought . . . Amy was kind of a pest . . . but they really cared about each other underneath, kind of like they were trapped between love and . . . well, being annoyed with each other anyway. And then they got trapped again between life and death and it like showed them that they really loved each other really. So we were capturing all the feelings of the book—everything Amy and Erin felt about each other—by acting out a scene.

Throughout the creation, rehearsal, and performance of this scene, Janne focused not on plot, but on the two main characters' feelings and what deeper thematic meanings these feelings imply. Libby, through our previous drama work, had done very well in evoking a story world she could see and in taking up various relationships with characters in that world. She had begun to bring and connect some of her personal experiences to her reading, and in a more limited way, to connect her reading back to her life. As yet, however, I had little evidence that she noticed and filled textual gaps in a story (Eco's points b, c, and d) and also no evidence that she was aware of and considered how she constructed meaning as she read.

Libby reported that what she liked about dramatizing this scene was that "it made it kind of come alive for me." She said that she had originally read the book, "just like a story—of what happened—without the feelings. [But after dramatizing the scene] I see that the whole meaning of the book was in the feelings. . . . I think drama is really good at feelings. I kind of started to feel like I understood the story when I started seeing the feelings." Here, Libby considers deeper thematic meaning and sees that she is "understanding" the story on a deeper level than that of the plot.

At this point though, Libby, still being more tied to the story landscape of action, felt that something was missing from their book report. In Bruner's (1986) terms, she was tied to the plot of the story instead of to the landscape of consciousness. As such, she was not pulled by the possibilities and personal potentialities of the story facts into "what those involved in the action know, think or feel, or do not know, think or feel" (p. 14). Libby therefore argued that they needed to do a scene from the book "so people will know what happened, what went on before and everything." She proposed to do a scene when the girls had a fight or disagreement. Janne immediately saw that "it's a good idea. It will make the feelings of the death scene more real."

Janne then had another idea. In the book, Erin, after understanding her sister's imminent death, writes an essay about Amy and what she likes about her. Janne proposed to start their performance with Erin reading the essay after Amy's death, "like she's trying to remember her good points" and then to do the scenes and then to end with Erin's reading the rest of the essay aloud. "Kind of like a flashback."

Libby didn't like that the order of the drama would not follow the order of the book. Janne explained that their purpose was to help people understand the book. "If you get them thinking about Amy dying—everything will make more sense. We have to help them get into it."

In the end, the girls introduced the essay, went back in time to role play a bedroom fight, dramatized the impending death scene, and then had Erin read the essay. After her reading, Erin answered questions in an interview about her feelings.

During this interview, Janne, in imagination, begins to realize implications of the text.

"The hardest thing was touching my sister one last time while her skin was warm and she was still breathing but she wasn't awake for me to say goodbye."

In answer to another question, she replied, "When you actually have the feelings of losing someone you love, you're filled with this feeling of being sorry for all the time you wasted and the times you were mean and didn't appreciate things. And I'm trying to make up for that now by appreciating what we had. I just wish we had done it when we had it."

Janne and Libby were both very excited by this particular dramatic collaboration. "I think we really understood what the author was saying," Janne said, once again revealing her penchant for getting at deeper meanings. "I see a lot of things I didn't see before," Libby revealed, "Things like feelings and little things that probably happened that I didn't see before. I mean, I never thought about why Erin wrote the story [essay] or how she felt later in her life. Now I think she will probably have a daughter of her own and name her Amy." Her drama work with Janne clearly helped her to enter into and to visualize the story, to begin filling in textual gaps, to go beyond the story, and to arrive at deeper meanings. She achieved a much deeper experience of the book through her drama work, and she helped Janne to a deeper experience and to a more constructed and artistically moving drama performance by bringing her back from the landscape of consciousness to the landscape of action, asking her to tie her experience of the text to the details of it.

A week later, Janne had this to share: "It depends how you read—what kind of reader you are—but lots of times when people read they don't capture that many feelings. They don't look in depth at feelings or how people look or move or say things. They just plain old look at the words. Drama captures all that stuff for people—it makes them use imagination like I do when I read."

When I asked Janne why some people only read words, she offered:

> I think they never learned how to do it. Like Libby, she can do it, but she doesn't know she's even supposed to or how to do it . . . she has imagination but she needs help to use it, to get it going. It's hard for her to see and feel what she reads so she would come over to me [during dramas or during free reading] and I would help her get going. Sometimes she'd say 'I don't know what to do' and I'd explain it—help her to get the picture, but I'd always do it as a character. And I'd want her to get into a character right away and to be feeling stuff and she would know what to do and would do it. She just needed a little push and she could go. I think drama makes you imagine everything, just like you have to when you read. . . . That's one thing I really like about the dramas—I can show her what to do, and I don't think I could really explain it to her without the drama, do you know what I mean? For other people, they just don't get it, or they don't have the time, or they don't care . . . it's just an assignment to get done. Drama is probably good for them too—it makes them slow down and think about things.

READING MORE REFLECTIVELY

Although Libby had indicated little interest in either theatrical performance or classroom drama before this school year, she quickly developed a remarkable facility for using it. Early in the year, drama helped her to enliven text and created a context in which she could receive assistance as she created story worlds with others both with and without the framing I provided as a teacher. Drama had become part of her meaning-making repertoire, which she used independently to deploy various new strategies for reading and constructing meaning, especially for connecting her life experience to her reading and vice versa. Towards the end of the year, drama continued to help her grow as she began to make more reflective moves for considering the deeper meanings of her reading experiences.

During a class reading of *Roll of Thunder, Hear My Cry* (Taylor 1976) toward the end of the school year, Libby's use of drama supported several new moves on reflective dimensions of reading response. During the first chapter, the Logan children walk to school on a rainy day in Depression-era Mississippi. The whites' school bus runs these children of color off the road and into a muddy ditch, much to the delight of the white children and to the displeasure and indignation of the Logan children. I asked my students to create statue pantomimes of the Logans that would capture their impressions and reactions to the events in the chapter.

Libby chose to be Big Ma, the children's grandmother. She stood with her hands on her hips, biting her lip as she watched the muddied children come home. Libby revealed that "Big Ma's kind of angry at first, but she kind of knows what's going on—that it's not the kids fault. So she's frustrated, but tries not to be mad at the kids . . . it's kind of like with my brother and he makes me mad sometimes even though I know it's not his fault I have to babysit him and stuff like that so I try not to be mad at him. . . . If this thing happens right off, then I think there's gonna be a whole lot of trouble in this book, and maybe Big Ma knows that and that's what she's thinking."

Here Libby brings her own life to literature and what she experiences with literature back to her life. She makes predictions and indicates a sense of wholeness and coherence from the very start. These kinds of moves were unthinkable for Libby earlier in the year.

Later in the book, she and Janne created their own missing scene drama by imagining, with some glee, what might have happened when Lillian Jean Simms—who was secretly beat up by Cassie—goes to school without her omnipresent "little black friend" serving her. Libby proposed that the boys she liked might snicker at her black and blue face, but Janne reminded her that Cassie had been careful not to mark Lillian Jean's face. They then concentrated on the reactions of her girlfriends who noticed Cassie was no longer hanging around, and Lillian Jean's embarrassment at having to explain. Although I did not witness the discussions or role playing of this scene, Libby described it with glee, taking obvious pleasure in the imagined comeuppance of the overbearing and racist Lillian Jean. With Janne's help,

Libby was noticing textual gaps and accepting the author's invitation to fill them. Drama had become such a natural and enjoyable meaning-making activity for the girls that Janne's mom reported to me during this time that the girls often role played when talking on the phone!

At the end of the book, all students participated in performing a *symbolic story representation* of a favorite scene, and in a group *newscast* about the book and TJ's (a boy of color framed for a robbery and murder committed by two white boys) upcoming trial—which is only hinted at in the book.

In both dramatic activities, Libby demonstrated that she was working to complete the experience of the text by bringing her life experience to the reading, filling gaps, and considering deeper meanings.

In a symbolic story representation, readers create cutouts or find objects to symbolize story characters, forces, and ideas, and also to indicate the setting, themselves as a reader, the author, motifs and themes. The reader then dramatizes the scene and her reading of it through the positioning of the cutouts and accompanying explanations (9). The important elements and process of reading a particular scene are therefore made visible through the performance.

Libby chose the final scene with the fire in the cotton fields as the topic for her representation. Libby used her reader cutout to show that at the beginning of the scene she was positioned with Cassie, Little Man, and Christopher John on the porch of the house, " and I was wondering so wildly what was happening to everyone" because the lives of Stacy and TJ and the safety of the farm and firefighters hung in the balance. When Cassie ran into the smoking fields, "I felt like I rose up in the sky and I could see everything from up in the air, and I felt like I could see what had happened in the night as much as I could see what was happening now . . . then I was back on the ground again." Here, I noticed for the first time that Libby had developed some awareness of how she read and how she positioned herself in a story.

At the end of her performance, she had a cutout representing the meaning of the scene, of which she said, "I think the central focus [a term we used in class for deep meaning] here is like the central focus of the book all together. It's like that sometimes you can't win, but you win by not losing. You can keep the people trying to beat you from winning." Indeed, Papa and Mr. Morrison had started the fire to save the lives of TJ and Stacey from the night riders and had achieved their end, even though they had sacrificed some of their cotton crop to do so. Again, this move to understand the deeper meaning of a story was relatively new for Libby, and certainly one that was assisted through the use of drama-oriented methodologies.

During their newscast, Janne and Libby explored how they thought the racism of the south would keep TJ from getting a fair trial, and also how the Logan family would stick together and continue to resist the assaults on their dignity "by hanging together and fighting back but only when they had to."

THE CHORUS COMMENTS

In a ritual we repeated several times during the year, my students were to enter class on Friday with their free-reading book and proclaim "I am a reader!" Earlier in the year, Libby had participated quite reluctantly in this ritual, but during our final free-reading Friday, excited by a video-taped drama she, Janne, and another classmate had made about the book *Meet Addy*, Libby gave me a stinging high-five and called out with a bit of a swagger in her voice, "I *am* a reader!" The subtext was clear: And you had better believe me!

At year's end, Libby said that language arts had become her favorite subject because of drama. She said that she felt "more equal in a drama. People listen to me more," and that reading after a drama "is different . . . I can see things better and I feel like I have more choices, just like in the drama." Over and over, Libby emphasized that she could do things as a reader, just like in a drama, and that she could exert control over her reading strategies. This was in direct opposition to the passive and submissive (Smith 1992) attitudes toward reading she had expressed earlier in the year. Drama had foregrounded her as a producer of text. Many teachers, including myself and Janne, had used the drama as a way of accompanying her into metaphoric worlds where we invited her to generate meaning and collaborated with her in creating that meaning through generative action, talk, images, and writing that were associated with the text and with the drama.

She was able to do so because drama had helped her, in Smith's (1992) terms to "merge" with and "enter" a textual experience and world. Once there, she used drama-related techniques to move around in this world, to observe, and to reflect upon it.

In fact, Libby revealed that she used her drama repertoire to read in other subject areas and with expository texts. "Even in a science book, I pretend about molecules, about being a scientist, discovering things, going into space . . . . Reading is plain if you don't have characters . . . an author needs characters to give ideas. So if there aren't characters I pretend to be one anyway, like I pretend I'm a scientist's helper and I'm doing an experiment. They're [the scientists] gone or something and I have to give the speech [about their findings] and it's got to be alive. I try to understand what things look like, how it works [she creates a mental model] like a rocket working—and then where it would be or be used [she creates a story world to contextualize the mental model] like going to Mars or something and I imagine I am giving a speech about it."

Drama undoubtedly made a whole new conception of reading available to Libby, and a whole new set of moves to go along with it. She often "tried on" the moves of more proficient readers like Janne that were made visible to her through the dramas.

In any case, the use of drama helped Libby overcome her local-level decoding focus and to begin creating global meanings that were personally relevant.

Drama gave Libby multiple forms for accessing her relevant experiences and applying them to her reading. Story worlds were created through drama, as the work established particulars of setting, time, and mood. Drama positioned her as a character and helped reading come alive, making the possible motives and psychology of characters available for examination. Drama made multiple voices available to her as she created meanings; this helped her to see that texts have multiple versus single meanings. Drama gave her real reading experiences to reflect on by establishing a focus and by giving her a lens for reading below the surface meanings.

Drama, it might even be argued, had generated the possibility for Libby to transact with literature. Drama had generated multiple possibilities for Libby to become a reader and to say with conviction "I *AM* a reader!", a member of what Frank Smith calls "the club of clubs." For me, as a teacher, that's what I call real-life drama.

NOTES

1. See Benton (1983) on "secondary worlds"; also Langer (1984,1989), Purcell-Gates (1991), Wilhelm (1997). Benton (1983) describes reading as the creation of "secondary worlds" and the involvement of the reader in creating, enacting, and feeling the text as "dramatic activity." Harding (1937, 1962) and Britton (1984) argue that readers must take on "the participant stance" to position themselves inside the world of a story, experiencing and elaborating on that story from within. These theorists also describe the flip side of "participating" as the "spectator role" in which the reader sees the text as an object in order to evaluate and reflect on it.

2. According to Bruner (1986), the reader must enter the textual world to "participate in story action" and enter a "landscape of action" that is directly stimulated by the facts of the story. Story entry and dramatic participation are necessary precursors to engagement on "the landscape of consciousness" in which the reader is pulled by the possibilities and personal potentialities of the story facts

into "what those involved in the action know, think or feel, or do not know, think or feel" (p. 14) (*see also* Thomson 1987).

3. Patricia Enciso's work on engagement (1990) describes engaged readers making various moves to enter story worlds and once there, taking on various roles, visualizing scenes and situations, and connecting text to their own real world experience. These are implicit prerequisites to learning from text. She describes engagement in reading as

   . . . our entry into the world of the story and the intense involvement we feel as we imagine and interpret the characters, setting, events, and thematic possibilities of literary texts. It includes a complex interplay of imaginative and intellectual processes that are typically private and elusive, yet critical to comprehension and pleasure in reading. (p. 1)

4. Less proficient readers have also been shown to read more slowly and less accurately than more engaged readers because they read in local, piecemeal ways and focus solely on cracking the code of the text. They do not bring extratextual information like their personal experience or theories of the world, known as schematic knowledge, to bear on the construction of meaning as they read. Neither do they use larger units of intratextual information like a sense of plot development, idea patterning, or coherence to aid in the creation of larger understandings. (Cromer 1970; Daneman and Carpenter 1980; Perfetti and Lesgold 1979).

5. This is something that Rosenblatt (1978) and other literary theorists (e.g., Iser 1978) make clear: reading is a transaction, a "compenetration of reader and text," and the "text" or reading itself occurs between the reader and book—a result of the conversation between them. Smith (1978) insists that reading is a highly social, purposeful, and meaning-creating activity. He stresses the importance of what a reader brings to the page, a body of background experiences he calls "nonvisual information." He writes that (179) "There is only one way to summarize everything a child must learn in order to become a fluent reader, and that is to say that the child must learn to use nonvisual information efficiently when attending to print."

6. See Barnes 1986; Knapp, Stearns, John and Zucker 1988; Rosenblatt 1978; Schank 1990; Vygotsky 1978; and Wade 1983.

7. David Booth is a pioneer in the use of story drama. His *Drama Words* (1987) and *Improvisation: Learning through Drama* (1985) have been a great inspiration to me; an even greater inspiration is seeing this formidable educator at work, which I have been privileged to do through some informally produced videotapes. His most recent work, *Story Drama* (1995), is a "must read" for anyone interested in drama and reading.

8. "The entire group of teacher and students must share both verbal and written text so the sharing is intermental. Simultaneously, these meanings must be internalized for each member and become the stuff of the thought system for each individual. That which is first social becomes psychological in the higher cognitive processes of each member . . . There is mutual participation by teacher and

children in the task, rather than the children performing while the teacher observes . . . Learning takes place in a mode of enterprise engagement; that is, children and teacher actually engage, in whole-task form, in the enterprise that is to be learned, rather than the teacher trying to teach small out-of-context pieces of the task or rules for how to go about it" (Tharp and Gallimore 1988). (Also see Goodman 1985; Jordan 1981a, 1981b.)

9. For background on the development of the technique, *see* Enciso, 1990, 1991; for descriptions and illustrations, *see* Wilhelm 1996, 1997.

3

Ethical Imagination:
Choosing an Ethical Self in Drama

Brian Edmiston

The really amazing thing is that we all saw it the same way. I mean, it never even occurred to me to look at it from the Indians' point of view. And it was hard to do, I kept saying 'No' to it and when I finally did [see from the Taino Indian point of view] it just blew my mind.
　　　　　　　　　—Luz, 7th grade girl, during the Columbus Drama

What should we do with the prisoners? They should go off in the spaceship with the aliens. It doesn't matter if they die, they're worthless anyway.
—Ron, 7th grader, as a Senator on day one of the Space Trader Drama

I've changed my mind. You can't decide for people. Even if we need the money we can't make them go—they're people too . . . and [even though they are criminals] we have to consider their families and their feelings and what's really fair.
—Ron, 7th grader, as a Senator on day four of the Space Trader Drama

Jeff and I share an ethical vision of education that affirms students' relationships with others as integral to their individuality. We agree with Noddings (1984) who argues that "caring" is our "basic reality." She be-

55

lieves that teachers ought to promote the formation of each student's "ethical self," which "is born of the fundamental recognition of relatedness; that which connects me naturally to the other, reconnects me through the other to myself" (1984, 24, 51). Carol Gilligan, in a similar vein, advises us to nurture webs of relationships "that revolve around a central insight that self and other are interdependent" (1982, 74). We both work hard in our classrooms—often failing, but never quitting—to build and maintain relationships among students and teacher in an atmosphere of care toward others and the world, which is engaging yet safe, demanding yet fair, challenging yet respectful.

We accept the ethical responsibility of this position—as we work and play with students we may either extend and strengthen or shrink and weaken the circles of care and connection that form with and among students. As Mimi Chenfeld has put it, every teaching moment is "either life or death, either opening up or closing down, either connecting or disconnecting"(1). We have both experienced the opening up to life which can happen in drama—the powerful caring circles that may be forged when students' imaginations are harnessed together.

Though *conflict* is at the heart of drama, in classroom drama the conflict must be between *ideas and views*—not between students (2). Paradoxically, though students can imagine all sorts of relationships, even hateful ones, drama work should create an atmosphere of care. Students may imagine that they assassinate another (as in the "Castle drama"—*see* Chapter 1) or they may make hurtful racist remarks (as in the "Roll of Thunder drama"—*see* Chapter 2) but these should be unifying not divisive experiences. Ideally, in drama students come to understandings *together* about why human beings kill or are racist—and about how we are *all* capable of killing or being racist (3). Some students may make profound discoveries about their prejudices or presumptions. However, the process of social- and self-discovery that drama can enable is not a cloak for meanness, for exposure, or for humiliation. As Dorothy Heathcote has continually stressed, drama "protects students into experiences" so that they are safe to imagine, explore, and confront possible ways of being in the world. At the same time, drama is a site for celebration of our humanity in the face of human—and inhuman—adversity.

When I first visited Jeff's classroom in the winter of 1994–95 (to work with Jeff and his students in the "Space Traders Drama" which is discussed later in the book) I was immediately struck by the friendly, respectful atmosphere. Having talked with Jeff over the two years since he had first used drama, I was expecting a classroom in which students cared about each other, their teacher, and their work. I was not disappointed. Within a few minutes I had seen Jeff joke with students, listen carefully, gently but firmly cajole them about incomplete assignments, and smoothly help them make the transition from a chaotic mass of adolescence into an attentive audience to his sharing of the day's plans. Within the next forty-five minutes, the students had laughed, listened to each other, cooperated, read, written, shared honest opinions, and left to do research in the library. I realized that students felt safe in his classroom and I understood why he had previously been able to explore ethical issues so productively with his students (in the "Columbus Drama"which is outlined later in this book).

When I work with students, I want us all to be open to difference and tolerant of diverse views whatever their source. I want us to listen for the silenced, to talk with the powerless, to see beneath the stereotype, and to hear above the rhetoric. I want us to listen for new voices, to continue to question, to argue, to rage, to laugh, and literally to make up our own minds. Drama is integral to my process of working towards these goals.

Jeff has similar hopes. When I asked him to summarize his ethical stance as a teacher, he wrote: " I hope to help students become responsible stewards for our fragile planet, help them to respect and celebrate diversity—and to know that diversity always leads to strength and vitality. I hope to assist them to become responsible democratic workers and citizens, provide tools for recognizing and correcting our human errors, and help them to become visionaries who use symbols to explore, express, and eventuate new, more humane ways of living together" (4).

As teachers, our ethical principles shape both what we value or encourage as well as what we question or disallow in daily classroom interactions. For example, my principle of caring means that I will not allow students to be disrespectful or hurtful toward each other in class. My knowledge of play leads me to encourage the use of drama to explore issues.

Students must be respectful, yet within a drama world, students can interact as if they are otherwise; they can imagine disrespectful or hurtful actions—they can also imagine caring and kind ones. The difference between imagined actions and actual ones is the subtle but profound difference between play and actuality. Players of any age, whether in the theatre or in a preschool, know when they are pretending and they want to play—they know they are not actually a king, actually restoring a castle, or actually being mean. The need for a trusting and safe classroom community is hopefully now quite clear: it is a prerequisite for a playful space in which students can imagine the worst—and the best—of humanity. Drama creates spaces in which students can explore the moral dimensions of the situations they read about and encounter on a daily basis in the classroom. Within a caring community in drama it is safe to explore less caring ethical attitudes toward others outside the classroom: for example, people who are or have been demonized, silenced, or treated as scapegoats.

ETHICS AND EDUCATION

We argue that teachers should promote the formation of students' "ethical selves" because no matter what or how we are teaching, a moral dimension and an ethical subtext are always present in our work (5). Peter Singer makes it clear: "We cannot avoid involvement in ethics, for what we do—and what we do not do—is always a possible subject of ethical evaluation. Anyone who thinks about what he or she ought to do is, consciously or unconsciously, involved in ethics" (Singer 1991, v). We agree. We want students to think about what they, and others, ought to do as they read literature, study science, or explore history. Rather than avoid moral issues, we believe that when they are relevant to curriculum issues and students' lives, ethical dimensions should be faced and confronted in the classroom, especially through drama (6).

In advocating the development of an ethical self, let me be clear that we are proposing neither moral indoctrination nor a moral vacuum in schools. The public school classroom is not a place for "politically correct" or rigid moral positions, which may never be formally stated but which students cannot seriously question. Nor is the classroom a site for the uncritical airing of any intolerant attitudes.

Bakhtin's Views of Ethics

Bakhtin proposes a radical middle path between the extremes of moral relativism and moral absolutism—a "prosaic" view of ethics based on *dialogue, imagination,* and *answerability* (7).

In genuine "dialogue," we imagine how the world looks from another's perspective at the same time as we see from our own point of view. Now we see the world with "double consciousness" (*see* Chapter 1) and as we act, or contemplate action, we do so in dialogue by keeping both this other's viewpoint in mind as well as our own.

Unfortunately, dialogue is less prevalent than you might expect. Much conversation and thinking are what Bakhtin calls "monologic" rather than "dialogic." Classrooms are no different when students' "opinions" are sought and expressed but not critiqued. Thoughtful dialogue—in which views are reconsidered and reformed—stands in contrast to what Deborah

Tannen (1994) calls the "triumph of the yell," which is unfortunately too often touted in popular media as a desirable outcome of an encounter between viewpoints.

Being "answerable" for our actions means that we acknowledge our agency within a specific context and particular circumstances—we are prepared to answer to other people who are affected by our deeds. In other words, we don't blame others and shift ultimate responsibility. Nor do we say that because we did not intend the consequences of actions, we are therefore not responsible for them. We are ethical when we recognize that as we act we are responsible for the consequences of our actions—from the other's point of view.

What Bakhtin calls a "prosaic" view of ethics grounds morality in the choice of actions by individuals who are in relationship with others at specific moments in time and space. In other words, ethics should never be wholly abstract—actions are always local and affect people in specific contexts. Considering how we ought to act means that we must always consider how the people who are going to be affected by our actions may view our deeds. We discover the other's views in face-to-face dialogue and in imagination as we try to see the context from their point of view. Though moral codes or policies will be influential, we are not ethical if we have an unquestioning reliance on either in order to determine how to act because any generalized or abstract principles cannot take into account considerations of a specific context.

If we are ethical in the ways Bakhtin outlines, not only will we have thought about how we ought to act but in doing so our initial opinions, points of view, and ethical understandings of issues will have been changed—the circles of connection with others will have been extended and strengthened and we will have *chosen* facets of an ethical self. In the classroom, this means that our understandings as teachers will change along with those of the students.

Drama and Ethics

Drama is a powerful tool for thinking about what we "ought to do" and uncovering some of the moral complexities of situations. Not only can students engage in *talk* about action—moral reasoning about what they *might* do if they were people in particular circumstances—in drama students take action and in imagination *do* that which in discussion they might only sketchily contemplate. As Jeff has shown in the previous chapter, students' talk about a book is very different from their acting as if they are the characters.

Dialogue Drama inherently involves talk as people interact. Yet the talk may not be genuine dialogue (or be dialogic) unless students imagine the world from another's point of view at the same time as they see from their own.

Some students imagine and dialogue with alternative viewpoints as they interact in daily life or in drama worlds. Even so, as Jeff discussed in the previous chapter, many students do not imagine situations from the positions of characters as they read. As will become clear in this chapter, even students who are "proficient" readers may not imagine alternative perspectives and positions to the ones they currently hold—whether they interact in drama or not.

Students do not just act in drama—they also *reflect* on the *meanings* of actions as they consider the consequences for different people. Reflection is dialogic when the students *evaluate* actions from the point of view of a person affected. Students can evaluate not only *others'* actions, but critically—for the development of an ethical self—in drama they can evaluate their *own* actions. Although we want students to judge peoples' actions and reactions to situations—and wonder what they would have done in similar situations—unless this leads students to reconsider their own positions and understandings, drama work, like so many classroom discussions, will merely reinforce whatever ethical assumptions the students bring into the classroom and express in their opinions (7).

Because interactions can be sequenced in drama—with students acting, reacting, and reacting again—students' dialogues in drama can be about the possible *consequences* of actions, which extend beyond those initially imagined and which complicate the students' ethical understandings of situations and issues. Planning and structuring so that this may occur in drama comprise what I call "dialogic sequencing" (8) (Edmiston 1994). The drama becomes dialogic when it is sequenced so that students' views—and as is discussed later, their discourses—in one episode are destabilized by their views and discourses in another episode; this can happen when they are brought into conflict in moments of drama encounter.

Answerability In drama, students take action as if they have become other people. They will be faced with being answerable for those actions if they view the consequences of the actions from the points of view of those affected. Participants in drama imagine from points of view that are different from their usual ones. Not only do students adopt roles that frame their relationships to situations, students view the world from different positions. Most significantly, in drama those who were regarded as *objects* of actions in one drama episode can become the *subjects* of action in another.

Prosaic Drama is most meaningful when participants contemplate specific urgent action rather than talk about generalities or abstractions. Students may formulate policy or acknowledge a moral code, but it is only when they apply principles in prosaic—or everyday—moments as they interact that they are being ethical.

Drama can create powerful dialogic spaces in which students' "ethical imagination" changes their moral understandings in making their views more multifaceted, interwoven, and complex. In the remainder of this chapter I describe and analyze two drama sessions in Jeff's classroom in order to explore in detail how this may happen.

THE COLUMBUS DRAMA

Jeff and his team teaching partner Paul Friedemann centered their teaching each spring on an integrated unit: "Social Issues and Civil Rights." During one week prior to this unit, Jeff used drama to introduce the unit as he applied and extended a lengthy drama session that I had devised and in which he had participated that semester in a university class. The drama revolved around the quincentenary of Columbus' arrival in the New World.

In Chapter 2, Jeff describes how a drama world brought the literary world of particular books to life. In this unit, drama worlds brought to life historical events that were described in the students' textbook and in works of literature, which Jeff also shared (9). The *missing scenes* approach was extended so that students imagined many other perspectives on events beyond those presented in the texts. Jeff used drama for about thirty minutes on five consecutive days. His students became captivated by the drama work, even though Jeff wisely paused in his use of drama both when he felt a need to plan his next teaching moves but also to give the students time to research questions that arose during the drama.

Jeff kept detailed notes of his teaching and retained mountains of students' writing and artwork. This unit was taught with five different classes—here I describe one. In this case, as at many other times, we talked a great deal about our teaching. I use Jeff's words to describe the moves he made in the classroom (Wilhelm and Edmiston 1998). The analysis of the teaching is both the result of an ongoing dialogue about the significance of our classroom work and a record of understandings I have articulated (Edmiston 1994, 1995).

Jeff wanted to challenge and problematize his students' related positions both on Christopher Columbus and on contemporary Native Americans. His students were mainly of European-American heritage. He had noticed that during the 1992 Quincentenary of Columbus, students seemed to be caught up in the popular conceptions celebrating Columbus as a cultural hero as they took part in school activities marking the event. He knew that mainstream academic knowledge echoed a view of Columbus "discovering" America and that students had encountered few, if any, challenges to this view in the popular media or in the school.

The students maintained that they were neither racist nor prejudiced, often insisting that they got along well with the small groups of minorities present in the school (Hmong immigrants, East Asians, and a few Native Americans, African Americans and Eastern European immigrants). Yet, at the same time, many students expressed very strong opinions regarding a "treaty rights" controversy involving local groups of Chippewa Indians and their rights to hunt and fish. They voiced mainstream ahistorical and acultural positions that treaty privileges were "unfair" to "sportsmen."

Swimming in Discourses

The notion that we live—and act—by "discourses" is critically important to a consideration of ethics (10). Everyone gradually acquires and accepts core positions that have a largely unseen effect as they shape and guide our actions and our attitudes about how we and others ought to act. Discourses shape our deep-seated initial points of view—and too often, our only views—on any issue. From the political arena to family life, our discourses are as integral to our opinions and interactions as the water is to the fish— we "swim" in discourses. We cannot avoid discourses; we encounter them and promote them every time we talk or read or watch television.

The students' historical views of Columbus and of contemporary treaty rights were discourses: from the comments Jeff noted and the opinions students expressed, it was clear to him that the students were swimming in the uncritical "mainstream" and were largely unaware of how little their understandings and attitudes had been unthinkingly constructed out of these discourses.

Unquestioned discourses work against the ethical need to be dialogic, answerable, and prosaic—to think and act and be responsible from more than one position in a context. We *may* critique our own discourses or embrace others' questioning approaches—and thus make them more dialogic. However, we tend to resist both our own and others' critical views because being unsettled about the ways in which we think may feel too much like undermining who we "are." One reason why drama is so powerful at disturbing our discourses is because when students express and critique discourses in imagination they feel safe because they are "just pretending."

Discourses are formed over time. For example, my commitment to "caring" is one of my discourses of "education," which have been formed over years as a teacher as I have experienced, created, read about, and reflected on classroom communities. My views on caring communities are not just theoretical positions but are discourses that get played out in every classroom interaction. Watching my silent and orderly classroom as a young teacher, you would have seen a very different type of community because I initially—and unsuccessfully—operated according to the authoritarian discourse that I had experienced as a child and that was the norm in the school where I first taught. Whereas now I act to connect with others, then I acted to distance myself from students; whereas now I seek out differences of opinions, then I was easily threatened by them. However, I was largely unaware of how my actions and attitudes were shaped by the "norms" that I had internalized and in which I swam. Although I began to challenge these norms as I experimented with innovation in my classroom, I did not radically begin to alter my practice until I encountered a brilliant teacher (Dorothy Heathcote) and a powerful teaching methodology (drama), which challenged my discourses.

I believe that it is part of a teacher's responsibility to challenge discourses respectfully—to make them more dialogic. We do so when we debate topics or discuss books—we raise questions, draw attention to inconsistencies, and highlight implications. James Banks (1993) argues that it is the teacher's responsibility to question discourses that promote inequitable views—to rework mainstream knowledge so that it becomes "tranformative." Discourses like "Columbus as hero," "manifest destiny," "Indians lose, superior culture wins" can then be problematized. Yet, in questioning positions we need to remain respectful and not tell students that their initial views are wrong. We also need to remain open to having our own discourses unsettled by students' views.

Drama that is dialogic is a powerful tool in pursuit of an objective of challenging discourses. Our purpose is not to "discover" the right way to look at an issue, but to "uncover" fresh perspectives, explore new points of view, and, in dialogue, forge new ethical understandings.

For me, good teaching must problematize and complicate initial views of a topic. If learning is a life-long journey, then classrooms are campgrounds and teaching opens new vistas for students and helps them consider new meanings of the journey's purposes. As students—and teachers—we are always in particular positions on different paths but these continually change as we walk, skyrocket, float, grope, dive, and swim our way through life. If we dialogue with other travelers, we will see the world in fresh ways. As we climb academic mountains, we have more panoramic views; as we lose ourselves in the forests of books, we emerge with fresh perspectives.

One way in which drama is "magical" is that we can not only imagine additional paths, destinations, and travelers, but also alternative worlds and worldviews to explore in dialogue. In drama, we are released from a single "opinion" and can explore alternative possibilities. In drama not only could we fly in the sea or swim in the air—in drama, students can become aware that they actually are flying or swimming. Dialogic drama draws attention to discourses and place participants in active—rather than reactive—positions relative to them.

Columbus Drama—Day One

Jeff used drama for about thirty minutes on the first day of the unit. Jeff's descriptions are in italics; analysis is in roman type.

> *I opened the drama by convening a Museum Board Meeting. In role as curator, I asked the board to consider renaming the Museum of American Culture as the Museum of American Cultures. A brief discussion followed, during which small groups of students considered and reported on their thoughts about the appropriateness of this proposed change. My purpose was to see how they defined culture and how they felt about the notion of multiple American cultures. Luz, reporting from her group, said they had discussed the idea of America as "a melting pot," and felt that there was one American culture, not many cultures. Her group proposed "keeping the old name."*

Note how students articulated mainstream discourses of "American culture." Even though the drama gave the students the opportunity to explore an alternative, they did not do so.

> *I attempted to problematize their decision by revealing that the museum had been given a generous grant to set up an exhibit on the topic of "Columbus and His Legacy" but that the donor wished us to consider changing the name of the museum in recognition of her gift.*
>
> *The students, in role as museum trustees, wanted to know who the donor was. I insisted the donor was anonymous but asked who they thought might give such a gift. Luz, for one, thought the donor must be "a minority person" who "wants to use the museum," presumably to present a particular political agenda. The students asked if we had to change the name of the museum to accept the money. When I said no, they quickly agreed to take the money but not to change the name of the museum. "Our job is to present history the way it was, not do any old exhibit the way someone wants us to do*

it," Tim said. I framed a brief discussion about political donations and whether donors had a right to expect favors. Luz differentiated between political donations and those given to a "museum like ours that is supposed to be neutral." The trustees agreed to staging a Columbus exhibit, but insisted that they be allowed to do it their own way. One girl said, "we're not supposed to rewrite history or anything."

Jeff, as curator, pressed the students, as trustees, to reconsider their position. They opposed him and questioned the motives of the donor. The direct conflict between the trustees' views and the curator's views did not lead to a change in the students' positions but revealed these more starkly within a discourse of history which seemed to be shared—that history is "neutral," that there is a single authoritative viewpoint which can be "told," and that revisionism, or "rewriting history," is wrong. There was talk but no dialogue.

I suggested, as curator, that I could use the trustees' help in brainstorming some ideas for our new Columbus exhibit.

Small groups began to brainstorm, and they mostly considered items they wanted in the exhibit: films, paintings, pictures of Columbus, statues, a replica of his ships, a computer game, maps, products Columbus "discovered" like gold and corn. Luz wanted a tabletop map placed next to a globe to show how Columbus' voyage had changed human conceptions of the world. Tim wanted contemporary letters and journals. When Joe suggested including Indian artifacts, I jumped on this and asked the trustees what they thought of including Indians in the exhibit. There was some disagreement. One boy thought we should have a scene of the Indians welcoming Columbus. Luz indicated that we should be concerned with the story of Columbus, and that anyway, we probably couldn't find real Indian artifacts. The group quickly dismissed the Indian issue and continued to talk about Queen Isabella, Columbus' childhood, cities in America named Columbus, and other issues.

I thanked the trustees for their ideas and asked them to step back and consider the theme and title of the exhibit. Luz called out "The Beginning of America." Tim thought "The Courage of Columbus" had a nice ring. Others were interested in the notion of "Discovery." The students decided on the theme of "The Discovery of America." I thanked them and ended the first day's drama at that point.

Jeff was keen that the students consider the point of view of the indigenous Taino people who were affected by the arrival of Columbus in ways the students had not considered (11). He amplified one boy's apparent interest in an indigenous view but wisely allowed the students to dismiss this concern. Instead, they continued to clarify their initial points of view: a European view on the first voyage of Columbus and a historical view of "real" Indians.

As Jeff noted, in Lisa Delpit's (1993) words, at the end of the first session the students had not demonstrated a willingness "to learn to be vulnerable enough to allow our world to turn upside down in order to allow the realities of others to edge themselves into our consciousness."

Columbus Drama—Day Two

On day two of the drama, I asked the students, in the role of filmmakers, to help create short films for one of the exhibits. I asked small groups to each use the tableau *strategy to show a scene they felt was important to put in the exhibit. Each group presented its tableau to the group using the related strategy of* forum theatre. *Each group acted out its scene. In some, the characters spoke; in others the scene was accompanied by a* narrative. *The rest of the class, as audience to these tableaux, offered advice about how to reposition the figures, recast action, and made suggestions for rewriting dialogue or narrative. All of the scenes had to do with Columbus planning his journey (meeting with Queen Isabella), undertaking the voyage (standing at the prow of the* Santa Maria *gazing confidently at the horizon) or arriving on the soil of the New World. Luz's group showed Columbus planting a cross and Spanish flag on the beach while an Indian knelt on the ground at his feet. Their narrative included the words, "I, Columbus, have sailed the ocean and discovered this country. I claim it now for Isabella, Queen of Spain. I bring civilization and religion to all people here!" The Indian whispered, "Oh, thank you, most powerful white man!"*

In a new role as historical consultant, I praised the artists for their work, but said, "You have told only part of the story. Your job is to tell the whole story! Whose voices are missing?"

Students called out: the sailors, the sailors' families, King Ferdinand, the family of Columbus, the Indians. I asked the students to respond as one of those who we had not heard from yet. Since they could not, I told them we would leave the drama and asked them what we needed to find out to continue the drama. In response to their queries, I made copies of primary source materials from diaries and historical accounts from Columbus, his sailors, and various people such as priests who accompanied him on his voyages. I also copied a chapter from Morning Girl *and made some copies of the book available.*

The students' shift in role to filmmakers framed them with a reason to show historical moments with motion and dialogue. As actors in the films, the students were not merely talking about what they would have done if they had lived at the time of Columbus, here they were actually doing what they imagined.

Further, as an audience to the performance of scenes, other students were in a position to *respectfully* critique them as fellow professionals. Even though there was plenty of talk, there was little apparent dialogue. The students continued to demonstrate the pervasiveness of their initial Eurocentric perspective.

Jeff honored their work but used the authority of his role to raise a key question—what voices did they think were missing from their views? He wisely ended the second session when the students found it difficult to switch perspectives.

Columbus Drama—Day Three

I began the next day using the analogy strategy. I had prearranged with one of the girls in class that I would pick up her journal and purse off her desk (12). As arranged, she protested. I said, "No, no. This is my purse and notebook now."

When several students protested, I continued to insist and said "I found it. Not only that, I found it in my classroom. It's mine."

The students quieted. I opened the purse and pulled out a note which I began to unfold. Several more students protested, including Luz. "You can't read her notes! That's personal!"

"Yes, I can," I persisted. "It's my notebook now."

"What makes you think it's yours," Luz argued, voice rising.

"It's mine," I said, springing the trap, "because I discovered it!"

Some of the students sputtered. "You didn't discover it," Luz almost yelled, "You stole it off of her desk!"

I acted incredulous. "Who thinks this is stealing?" I asked the class. All of them raised their hands.

"How can this be stealing?" I asked them, "when you say that Columbus discovered America?"

By this time, most of the students had read about Columbus's purposes in discovering the New World—to find gold for himself and to secure himself and his heirs as rulers of this New World. They had also read about many of the atrocities committed as the Taino Indians were forced into slavery, and mutilated and killed for their resistance or failure to find gold. The reading had described the ravages of smallpox on the Indians and their initial friendliness to the Spaniards, which was answered with nothing short of genocide. These things were described in primary documents by Spanish witnesses.

A very lively discussion ensued during which many students indicated confusion about why these things were not more widely known or studied. Luz lamented that her father even belonged to "the Knights of Columbus. I used to think it was cool—now I think it's disgusting! You think of knights in shining armor . . . but his knights killed all those people . . ." Some students doubted that the readings were true. Others shouted that the readings were "by the Spanish! Why would they lie?"

This episode displays the power of students being propelled into an experience of sudden dissonance. Note that the student whose journal and purse Jeff removed had previously consented to the move so that only other students would be momentarily incensed and she would not feel personally violated. The word "discover" was recontextualized in an event in which the preposterousness of Jeff's position was juxtaposed with the previously uncontested Eurocentric view of discovery and then connected to the viewpoints presented in the students' readings. The students' discourse on discovery was suddenly brought into relief by a point of view which they instantly adopted—don't touch other people's "stuff." Those who said they were "confused" probably experienced an unsettling in the discourse of discovery and were beginning to dialogue with themselves.

Note the danger of "flip-flopping" superficial views in the way Luz suggested she might have been about to do—from all "good" to all "bad." When students do not have a great deal of information about a topic and have only considered one or two viewpoints, a tendency exists to totally reject a previous assumption as new perspectives are considered. There is a danger of becoming as rigid about the "new" way of looking as they were about the "old." Instead, what we want to promote are "dialogic" views, in which students recognize that there are always new ways of looking at events.

In this context, it is important to stress that during the week students conducted extensive research on Columbus and viewed a videotape examining different perspectives on Columbus and his legacy. Students had the opportunity to read and view materials that ranged along a continuum of multiple viewpoints from those broadly "pro-Columbus" like *I, Columbus* to those "pro-Indian" like *Encounter*. Jeff was aware of the danger of emphasizing particular viewpoints and was explicit in making it clear that any historical information and all views were appropriate in drama and in discussion.

> *I asked the students to re-enter the drama world. As curator I observed that I knew they had been studying the history of Columbus and, referring back to the end of the previous session, I wondered if there were voices they wanted to add to the museum. The artists agreed that they wanted to tell the story of the voyage from the sailors 'viewpoint and of the Spaniards' arrival and its aftermath from the perspective of the Indians.*
>
> *To capitalize on this opportunity, I asked the students to pose as sailors or Taino Indians and create an interactive exhibit. When a visitor walked by, they would speak about their experience. The students worked in pairs to prepare and then formed a circle. As I walked round, in the way a visitor would, they shared their prepared lines. Tim was a sailor: "I ate hardtack filled with bugs. I thought we would fall off the edge of the world. And he promised us gold, and there is no gold!" Luz was an Indian, "We welcomed them. We were willing to share but they destroyed us. They brought greed and disease. My family is dead." Other sailors said, "I want to go home. Let us take what we can*

*and go home. This is no place for us," and were answered by Tainos who said, "Go
home and leave us in peace. This place was given to us by the Great Spirit. It is not for
you to rule or own!"*

By speaking as the "missing voices," the students saw from inside perspectives they had previously either not considered or only fleetingly adopted. As sailors and Tainos they could review everything they had read but from new positions. New experiences were imagined that both contextualized images of fears, promises, and death as well as problematized the discourses of discovery and Columbus. Those who had seemed to be marginal bystanders—sailors and Indians—now came to the center of the world of Columbus. Those who had been the *objects* of the actions of Columbus and his men now became the *subjects* of new actions. Students could "fall off the edge of the world" and see it afresh from where they landed.

As the students reflected on events from new positions they dialogued with previous positions, created new meanings about historical events, and evaluated the previous actions of Columbus and his men from the point of view of disgruntled sailors and peaceful Tainos.

There are always additional "missing voices" that could be explored through drama. For example, the views and evaluations of historical women or Jews, impoverished Spanish peasants, or those who had opposed the genocide would have been interesting to adopt; each would have raised further questions and offered new perspectives and positions for dialogue.

*We then all became Tainos, meeting in a circle as a tribe to share stories of what was
happening, and suggestions of what to do. Many of the boys wanted to fight, but were reminded of the Spaniards' superior weaponry and strength. Others wanted to send emissaries to explain our point of view, but we agreed the Spanish were "gold crazy." Some
decided to build canoes and escape to nearby islands, but recognized that this was only a
short-term solution. "There is really nothing we can do!" one girl agonized. That night, I
asked the students to write three diary entries as a Taino—one before Columbus' arrival,
one during his arrival, and one a year after his arrival.*

Now everyone in the class adopted the same Taino point of view. From this position they shared multiple interpretations and evaluations of how the native people might have reacted—from escape to violence to inertia. As the students dialogued, they critiqued their new views. In contrast to the encounter between Jeff and the students on the first day—here the students' energies were opposed not to what his role might intend but to a known common threat—the historical events after the arrival of Columbus and his men. Their discussion—and subsequent writing at home—focused not on rewriting history, but on an exploration of and dialogue about possible diverse reactions by the native people.

The work led the students to consider in depth the ethical dimension of how the Taino "ought" to have responded. Luz provided an illuminating response that clarified that, at least for her, for the first time she had imagined how a Taino had viewed the events. Her view was transformed from an external judgment of others' actions to holding two simultaneous insider points of view.

> *After this class, Luz responded that "The really amazing thing is that we all saw it the same way. I mean, it never even occurred to me to look at it from the Indians' point of view. And it was hard to do, I kept saying no to it and when I finally did [see from the Taino Indian point of view] it just blew my mind." Luz admitted that she was very "upset and confused" by what she had learned and experienced. "It's just so different from what I thought," she said, "it's hard to put together." When I asked her what had turned the tide, she said, "reading the descriptions helped. Morning Girl (the book she read from a Taino point of view) made me think of what life was like before Columbus came—how much that changed everything for the worse. And then being in the drama upset me because I felt so much like something had been taken from me! . . . and then when I heard all the other voices [in the drama, of sailors and Indians] it was like it was just drowning out all of the cool things I still believed yesterday about Columbus."*

Luz's response illustrates the dialogic power of adopting and interacting in drama from a novel point of view. Although she had read about Tainos and had even read a text written from a Taino point of view, it was not until she personalized the position by standing in the shoes of a native, speaking from her viewpoint, and hearing the situated voices of others, that she actually adopted the Taino perspective—it ceased to be "their" view and became another one of "her" views. The effect was clearly explosive, upsetting, and confusing as her discourses surrounding Columbus were "drowned" in a dialogue of new voices.

Columbus Drama—Day Four

> *At the beginning of the next class, the students exchanged diaries in the role of curators. I asked them, in their roles to consider the importance and effect of including such viewpoints in the exhibit.*

Jeff reestablished the museum context, thus framing the students with a professional historian's responsibility as they read and evaluated their own writing. The move that followed built on the writing they had done the previous night so that in the drama the students further contextualized and explored broader cultural discourses about life and beliefs.

We took on the perspective of Tainos who had found a small child floating in a canoe. As a shaman, I asked the students, as tribespeople, to offer what the child must learn to become one of us. Based on their recent research, the students said, "learn our language and customs." When I pressed them, Luz answered, "love of nature and respect for animals—for life."

"All life?"

"We are a peaceful people."

"What else?"

"Know about our beliefs?"

"Such as?"

"The Great Spirit, who provides all things. Being thankful for fire, water, food and other gifts."

We then proceeded to engage in a naming ceremony for the boy, during which each Taino would give the boy a secret name and a gift to signify what he must know and become to be a Taino. Luz gave the boy the secret name "Sunshine" and an eagle's claw to remind him "to enjoy the gifts of the Great Spirit and to never be greedy for more."

Here the students were developing discourses related to a "Taino" view of life. By enacting a naming *ritual* together they had a powerful shared experience and built a broadly common viewpoint. In doing so, some students used the opportunity to dialogue with previous positions *and* evaluate them. This is suggested in the ensuing ironies: the Tainos adopt a stranger as one of their own, whereas the Spaniards soon kill and enslave strangers; the desire not to be greedy is a gift that contrasts with the known effects of greed on the Spaniards and the Tainos.

We shifted the drama world to Spain in 1494 when Columbus was trying to fund a second voyage of 17 ships and thousands of people. This was difficult because the first voyage had lost money. The students became Columbus' emissaries to the King and Queen, attempting to justify the support of the King. Based on their reading, they spoke of trade routes, competition with Portugal, Indian slaves, Christianizing the world, gold and riches, settling new colonies, and more. In my role as King's courtier, I resisted all arguments, pressing them to explain themselves further. I eventually struck an agreement to Christianize all Indians and to bring a guaranteed amount of gold back to the King. (Both are historical facts.)

In this role, I asked the entourage of Columbus to develop a policy that I must approve for what to do when encountering new Indians. First, it was agreed that Indians must ac-

cept Christianity and that they must be enslaved to serve their new King. Historical wood-cuts were passed around that showed the Indians being hunted with dogs, having limbs chopped off for not bringing enough gold, being burned if refusing to accept the King and Christianity. "Do we have other options for dealing with these savages?" I asked.

As they clarified their policy, some students insisted that the Tainos must be made servants of Spain: "We must protect ourselves first." "Kill them if we must." "If we take everything from them then they must serve us."

The students used all the information they had gathered in their readings as they adopted the point of view of emissaries from Columbus. As Jeff, in role as a courtier, opposed them he pressed the students to think more deeply about some of the implications of the discourses of "trade," "religion," and "wealth," which underscored the Spanish expeditions.

Note how the *possibilities* for internal dialogue were opened up because the students already knew much of what was going to happen in the New World and had begun to explore Taino perspectives. Students *may* have dialogued with themselves very little and may have been more interested in imagining contexts of violence implied by discourses of colonization.

As the drama continued, other students resisted policies that condoned violence. Luz said, "I will not help you with this."

"You are no longer one of us—you are not a Spaniard," I told her, and she was made to turn outward from the circle. "They have rights too—they are human beings," said another student, who was also turned outward from the circle. "No, they are not," I replied, "they are savages in a land we have discovered!" We proceeded to discuss the differences between being civilized and being savages.

Jeff now used the authority of his role both to "ventriloquate" (in Bakhtin's word) positions which were historically held, and to impose consequences on actions. In doing so he illuminated the discourses of colonization that were in operation. By silencing public opposition, he pushed some students to fume—and dialogue internally—as others talked about discourses of "civilization."

In the next scene, which proved to be the climax of our drama, we divided into Spaniards and Tainos re-enacting the first landing of Columbus. The class was divided into halves that planned the re-enactment and then performed it for the other half of the class. That audience played the role of historians checking for historical accuracy against the documents we had read.

The drama has come full circle. The students have returned to the moment at which they began a week earlier. However, they are in a very different space because of all that they now know about this moment, which they discovered in their research, discussions, and through the drama. Again, note the extensive possibilities for genuine dialogue in this encounter. Now students can revisit their previously Eurocentric positions but in dialogue with problematized discourses of colonization as previously critiqued from Spanish and Taino perspectives. Knowing some of the consequences of the encounter—what will happen to the native people and the Spanish explorers—now puts students in a position of being faced with being answerable for whatever they say in the scene. This is especially so for those who represent the Spaniards.

> *In Luz's group, the sailors rowed up to the shore, jumped out of their boat and kissed the land, but immediately put up their weapons upon seeing the Tainos. The Tainos brought fresh fruit and yams and Columbus presented them with trinkets.*
>
> *Columbus: (plants flag) I claim this land for Spain. The soldiers then surrounded the Indians. "We have them, sir!"*
>
> *To this, Columbus ironically replies, "Tell them not to fear. We come in peace." To which Luz, as a Taino elder, replied, "Then why are we being guarded?"*
>
> *The Tainos were asked to pledge allegiance to the King of Spain. When they came to understand this demand, some did so and some resisted. The resisters were shot.*

Columbus Drama—Day Five

> *On the final day of the drama, we became the mountains on the island of Hispaniola. I asked the students to "stand and look at history. What stories do you want to tell?"*
>
> *After five minutes to prepare, we stood in a circle. Each student had his say and then tapped the next mountain. Luz started the poem by asking: "They dug out what little gold we had, and ignored the trees and birds. I wonder if it made them happy?" She was followed by students saying, "The Spaniards dug mines and filled them with bodies." "Peace was followed by war." "I was angry but could watch and do nothing."*

Adopting the inanimate perspective of the mountains framed the students with a distance that made them historians with a different responsibility. As nature's storytellers, they could look in from the outside on both Spanish and contemporary points of view to raise more philosophical critiques such as wondering if the Spaniards were happy.

> *To end the drama, we returned to our roles as curators creating the central exhibit. They decided to create a sculpture. As students entered the sculpture, each added onto what had previously been composed. First we had Columbus, pridefully planting the flag.*
>
> *Then we layered in the mountains shaking their heads at the great change to the peaceful island and covering their ears in distress. Sailors entered who tied up Tainos who cried to*

be released. Queen Isabella was placed at the far left with a cross in her hand, and the Taino chief at the far right praying to the Great Spirit. The caption read, "Columbus, who discovered a land for one civilization and destroyed the one that was already there."

Making the sculpture was a synthesizing aesthetic medium through which the students could reflect and transform into images some of the new feelings and thoughts that had arisen in their previous dialogues. Doing this together created a moment of unity in diversity—now multiple views coexisted not in narrative but in overlapping patterns.

Individual writing provided another medium for synthesis and reflection. Now students could step back from their experiences of and from different viewpoints into "their" position and consider how their views had changed. One student made a connection to contemporary Indian issues; others commented on the experience of the process.

In their reflective journal entries, one student wrote that "now I understand why the Indians [in Wisconsin] are so angry about the treaty rights thing." Another wrote: "It's interesting to think about things from different directions. I felt kind of like we held Columbus in our hand like a ball and turned him around to see all sides." Luz simply wrote: "Wow! That was intense!"

Dialogue is essential. Bakhtin says "To live means to participate in dialogue: to ask questions, to heed, to respond, to agree, and so forth." (Bakhtin 1984, 293). Drama *can* create the opportunities for ethical dialogue to occur—dialogue that can radically alter how students think about issues and their relationship to them and the people whose lives are or were affected by people's actions. In imagination, students can experience new viewpoints. In dialogic drama, students views can become both more troubled and clearer as alternative positions are adopted and explored in dialogue with each other. In drama, students can take steps on the path to creating more complex positions as they become more aware of how discourses both shape their lives but also how they can change those discourses and thus their views of their relationships with others. In drama, students can choose facets of an ethical self.

THE SPACE TRADERS DRAMA

When Jeff began the "Social Issues and Civil Rights" unit two years later, he invited me to come to his classroom. He was interested to see how through drama we could explore such ethical concerns as prejudice, racism, justice, and fairness. Like the students two years previously, his European American students maintained that they were neither racist nor prejudiced because of good relations in the school between them and the few "minority" students or those who were the children of recent immigrants. They did not recognize how discourses of, for example, prejudice operated in their lives despite individual cordial relationships.

I used drama for forty-five minutes with three of his classes back-to-back over three mornings; Jeff participated throughout and took on roles. In the afternoons, he worked alone with the two other classes. Broadly the same teaching moves were used with each class—I describe and analyze the teaching moves from one of the classes but record students' responses from several. As with the "Columbus drama," descriptions of each day are in italics with analysis in roman type.

I had been reading a short story, "The Space Traders" and thought that the central conflict might be a useful starting point for the class. The story comes from Derek Bell's collection *Faces at the Bottom of the Well*, which examines racism and prejudice in America. It is set in a future when the United States is approaching economic and environmental collapse. The government is near bankruptcy and desperately needs money in order to rebuild and restore the country. "Alien" people from another planet land on Earth and offer the government all the gold they need for economic recovery in exchange for all the African American people in the country. The short story ends with the offer being accepted.

Space Traders Drama—Day One

The first day began by asking students if they would take on the roles of people framed with responsibility for major national policy decisions. The students were interested and chose the roles of Senators. I took on the role of majority leader. (Other groups made different choices, for example, one group chose members of the Cabinet—I became the President's Chief of Staff).

I announced that an emergency session had been called because the country was facing economic disaster. The budget simply had to be slashed. The students brainstormed how this emergency was affecting the country and imagined, for example (in some classes they also showed these in tableaux), collapsing infrastructure, inadequate health care, and social unrest.

Small groups worked together to list everything on which the government spent money. When reports were made, we listed and categorized expenditures into budgetary items like the military, highways, parks, welfare, prisons, education, police and fire services, and many others. I then told the Senate that one whole budget item had to be eliminated, and that this would shortly be debated. They again resumed small group work to discuss what item should be eliminated.

The students were invited to enter and create a context similar to that of the short story. The students drew on and extended their knowledge of government expenditure to outline categories for initial thoughts about government social—and ethical—responsibility. The conflict of the drama (impending economic collapse) created a tension that demanded drastic action—budget cuts. In considering this action, the students had to prioritize and were forced to decide what was not "essential." Drawing on discourses about what is essential in society they were in a position to marginalize programs and thus the people affected.

> *When we reconvened, spokespersons from each group were invited to introduce themselves and their group's proposal for cutting a budget item. They enjoyed being, for example, "Senator Jones from the Great State of Idaho." When each group had made its presentation, a debate ensued. Several votes were taken before a decision was made. In three classes, it was decided to completely cut welfare; in another two classes, all prison services were cut.*

I had originally intended to establish a drama context similar to that in the story and as an "alien space trader" ask for African Americans in exchange for gold. However, what became clear was that each class was operating by mainstream discourses that marginalized other groups more strongly—those on welfare and those in prison. At this time, the U.S. House of Representatives was voting on massive public spending cuts and the students were surrounded by rhetoric in support of these positions.

> *In the next episode, the Senate was reconvened. I told them that a truly unbelievable event had occurred. We had been contacted by "aliens," who had offered to repair our ecosystem, fix our infrastructure, and provide us with billions of dollars worth of gold to support our economy. I reentered in role as the Space Trader and made my offer. In every class, the students almost immediately wanted to know the catch.*
> *"I want your least valued group of people to take with me back to my world."*
> *"Why?"*
> *"That is none of your concern."*
> *"What will you do with them?"*
> *"That is none of your concern."*
> *"Who do you think are our least valued citizens?"*
> *"You have already identified them," I ventriloquated, "they are the welfare recipients (or the prisoners)." I then echoed many of the arguments students had previously made for eliminating welfare (or prisons).*

After an intense interrogation, the Space Trader left, giving the senators "twenty-four hours before I take this offer to another nation."

There was an intense debate but few dissenting voices when the Senate voted overwhelmingly to accept the Space Traders offer.

We then used continuum and radio show strategies. The Senators were asked to write a press release for their home state outlining why they had opposed or supported this measure. They then lined themselves up in a continuum stretching from those who agreed most strongly with the decision to those who disagreed most strongly. To do this students had to consult and share their views with each other. Jeff came down the line as a radio talk show host interviewing Senators on the reasons for their decisions.

These strategies gave each student opportunities to express a personal ethical stance. Although they had agreed to go along with the majority, in their writing, in placing themselves bodily on a continuum, and in response to a question, each student had several opportunities to think through and state an individual position.

In his radio show comments, Ron said, "What should we do with the prisoners? They should go off in the spaceship with the aliens. It doesn't matter if they die, they're worthless anyway."

Nancy's press release read that "I believe we should cut welfare and send these people with the aliens. Is it our fault if people don't choose to work? Because they are too lazy!? Why is it our fault if they drop out of school? I believe people who are disabled should have it [welfare], because they had a reason, but it's not fair for the people who have to work their butts off for their own families to pay for people like this! Now they will be made to do some good for society [by going with the Aliens].

In an emotional and rare dissenting view, Bethany said, "I disagree with this! It is just like the slaves! We take people who are free and we're trading them again for money! Can't we see? When will it stop?" The girl next to her in the continuum said, "What? When will what stop?"

Bethany continued: "Mistreating people! It's just like the slaves! We have no right to do this!" The students paid close attention to Bethany, but at the end of the radio show, when we asked if people wanted to change their opinion and position on the continuum, no one showed by moving that they had done so.

Students like Ron and Nancy may have been experimenting with holding extremist positions—drama protects students into doing so because all serious contributions are legitimate. However, drama does more than allow students to voice racist or intolerant attitudes. In the drama, Bethany could challenge these positions. But there would be no ethical dialogue between them—and thus no significant change in position—unless students allowed different views to (in Bakhtin's word) "interilluminate" each other. Later episodes in the drama enabled this.

> *In the next episode of the drama, we asked students to take on the position of a welfare recipient through a step-by-step strategy. We began by asking students to kneel on the floor and close their eyes. Through* guided imagery, *we asked them to imagine themselves as adults with a dream home and a dream job. When they had done so, they were to commit to this vision by taking a step and once again kneeling. Next they were asked to imagine some kind of problem at work that caused them to lose their job, to take a step and kneel in that new position. In this way we took them through several trials and tribulations to the point that they registered for welfare. We then asked them to pair up and tell their story to a partner. (A similar process was used for those who committed crimes).*
>
> *For homework, we asked students to write two journal entries: one from the perspective of someone who had come to be on welfare, and another as "themselves" to reflect on the various reasons others might come to be on welfare, and what could be done to help people on welfare to improve their situations.*

The students' imagination was activated in the step-by-step strategy, the guided imagery, and the journal entries so that they could take up the perspective of people receiving government assistance and, in reflection, rethink their previous position. Those who had been objects now became subjects; it was much harder for the students to dehumanize "people on Welfare," to treat them as a homogenous group, or see them as "them."

> *Nancy, in contrast to her diatribe the day before, had this to say: "I just had a run of bad luck, and people were cruel to me, my boss wouldn't understand or help me . . . Is it a person's fault if they commit a crime—yes. Is it a person's fault if they don't have a job—not necessarily. Yesterday, I would have said that they chose [not to work] and that therefore we [as Senators] could take their power to decide for them. But now that I have been on welfare, I can see that it might not be a person's choice, in fact, it probably isn't and maybe no one is helping them to get a job and get on their feet again."*
>
> *Ron wrote: "I was a victim that got beaten up. And my family. And the police wouldn't help. When I took things in my own hands for revenge, the police caught me and put me in prison. Is this fair? And now I am going with the Space aliens."*

Students have made some significant shifts in their positions. Yet note how, as in the Columbus Drama, there is a danger of students "flip-flopping" their positions—from being completely individually responsible for what happens to not having responsibility. This would seem to be a product of dichotomous either/or thinking—something drama can alleviate if multiple views are explored.

Space Traders Drama—Day Two

On the next day, the students were again role playing welfare recipients (or prisoners) who had been put into a holding prison to await being handed over to the aliens. The class observed certain prisoners through "one-way mirrors" as they discussed their fate on their last night on earth. We also did television coverage, interviewing family members, political pundits, and people on the street about their views of the impending "space trade."

These strategies continued to humanize those who had previously been marginalized. Talking to relatives added perspectives that highlighted the financial, emotional, and social consequences if the people were allowed to go. These views were questioned by Jeff and me (as political pundits) and by students (as people on the street)—dialogue was occurring in the classroom for many students.

We then used tableaux in which small groups imagined the best possible scenario for the welfare recipients when they landed on the alien's planet. Ron's group imagined a kind of endless vacationland, sitting in the sun and being served by alien women. They provided the caption: "Like Winning the Lottery." Then they were asked to imagine and create an image of the worst possible scenario. Ron was laid out on an operating table, while alien surgeons harvested organs from his body for their research. Their caption read: "We are lunch meat to the Aliens." Nancy's group imagined a best-case scenario of being able to start a new human colony in space, and a worst-case scenario of being enslaved.

This strategy was used by the students to create images of possible consequences for the people who would be traded. In the first episodes of the second day, students had looked into the future to imagine what might happen.

When the groups were asked whether they would, of their own free will, be willing to risk the worst possible scenario to gain the best possible one, every single student voted no. They discussed at length the costs even of the best scenario—being permanently removed from family members, human company, and even missing more mundane human ceremonies and events, such as Ron's wistfulness at "not being able to catch the World Series or Super Bowl."

When the students reconsidered the present in the light of the future they radically altered their positions. A "present filled with its own future" is the unique dramatic experience (S. Langer 1953, 307). Because participants have to think of what might happen, they see their situation quite differently; although they are in the present, they are also in dialogue with their own images of the future. Those students who regularly create images of possible futures have learned to imagine likely consequences and to consider them as they consider possible actions. Those who do not can learn to do so through drama when they create and reflect on specific images, for example, through the tableaux strategy. Further, as they interact with peers and teachers, they can be assisted to imagine and consider more sophisticated and complex consequences as well as critique discourses that have previously been largely unexamined.

They once again became prisoners during their last night on earth. They were allowed to write one last letter. Most wrote to their families.
Ron instead elected to write to the Governor for leniency:

Dear Governor,
I really don't think you have the right to send us to another planet. My family thinks I am a good person even though I committed a crime. I think you should not send us if we are willing to work or if our family is willing to pay to take care of us. If a member of your family was in prison would you want them to leave this planet and never see you again? Would you trade people you should love and respect for money? Would you? Probably not because you'd never see them again. You don't have to do this, you know. You can still do the right thing and save us.
Sincerely,
A welfare person

Nancy wrote to the President:

Dear Mr. President,
I realize I do not have a job, but haven't you ever heard of someone making a mistake or having problems beyond their control?! Well I have but I've learned and I'm solving my problems. Now I'm being sent to outer space. My family is coming with me just because I'm going but I'm worried that my children won't get an education and will forget all about earth.
I didn't think this is what America was about but now I know that it's true. We were not all created equal. We'll take advantage of the weak as long as it doesn't hurt the strong. Also, do you realize you're not solving the problem, you are running away from it!
P.S. It's not fair. I have suffered for my problems that were not even my fault and now I am suffering a second time!

Ron, who had previously dismissed prisoners as "worthless," now saw worth in individual people who should be "loved" and "respected." He asked the governor to be ethical, "do the right thing," and imagine someone as a member of his family—something he had not done previously.

Nancy had previously regarded all people on welfare as at fault for being lazy—thus, they should not complain if they had to be sacrificed for the benefit of others who were hard working. In her letter, she repositions the "weakness" of those on welfare to see not wholly individual "faults" but social and power issues. She critiques the previous decision as an abuse of power by the "strong" and extends her argument to question the discourse of equality in American democracy.

Space Traders Drama—Day Three

On the final day of the drama, I entered as the warden to load up the welfare recipients (or prisoners) onto the alien spaceship. When Ron's group staged a sit-down strike and refused to board the spaceship, I adopted the position that Ron, Nancy, and other students had voiced earlier. "You're just worthless. I don't know why the aliens want you—you are dirty rotten criminals who don't want to work! You can't even follow the rules of society. You are scum!" The students, many of whom had spoken these exact phrases, were angry and retorted that "You've no right to talk to us like that!" and " You don't even know our stories!" Ron yelled, "Did you ever think of helping instead of kicking people who are down?" Among the welfare group, one boy said, "You know nothing about work. You've never lost your job!"

When students have previously expressed strong opinions these can be ventriloquated later in drama to create powerful moments of intense ethical dialogue. The teacher can adopt and present students with a position that they have previously expressed. In effect, the students then encounter and face themselves. Such forceful statements must be distinguished by the teacher in role from merely hurling such positions at students. The students are not trapped in a humiliating put-down, but on the contrary are in a powerful ethical position to critique their previous attitudes and thus the discourses which supported these views.

As our final episode, we reconvened as the Senate to reconsider our vote. After a debate, the Senate voted not to send the welfare recipients. In Ron's class twenty-five were against, with one still for the Space Trade and one abstention. When the Senators were interviewed by TV journalists about why they had made this sudden turnaround and how they were now going to solve the nation's terrible problems, Ron said, "I've changed my mind. You can't decide for people. Even if we need the money we can't make them go—they're people too . . . and we have to consider their families and their feelings and what's really fair. . . . I think we would just be causing more problems than we solved."

Later, in discussion the groups dealing with welfare discussed the complexity and justice of making people take jobs who had small children or who had trouble taking care of themselves. Although the students recognized that they could not find the solution, they did make various suggestions of how government policy could be changed to be more humane and yet solve the problems of helping everyone to engage in useful work.

In an incredibly trenchant discussion for a young adolescent, Nancy later admitted in an interview with Jeff that "I originally suggested this [Space Trade] but when you look at it from their [the welfare recipients'] point of view it's really different. I thought we could eliminate welfare by getting rid of the welfare people. Now I see that this is a big ill—not a personal ill. We'll still have the welfare problem because people will still be treated unfairly and people will still lose jobs and people will still have problems. It's not the people—it's human nature—it's society. Eliminating welfare isn't even the point to me now. The point is making it clear what we care about, how we want people to behave and how we will help them to do that before and when they have problems, because the problems will happen."

The final episode and the subsequent discussion provided opportunities for Ron and Nancy to further explore and clarify their new views and critiques of discourses. Ron decided that in this case he could not make a decision for someone else. Nancy continues to shift her ground from an individual view of the "problem" of welfare to a societal perspective, which revolved around a central ethic of caring.

CONCLUSION

Maxine Greene (1990) has succinctly stated that by "Naming, articulating, affirming the dissonances and contradictions in our consciousnesses, we may be able to choose ourselves as ethical in unexpected ways."

This chapter has illustrated how, in drama, teachers can assist students to discover both old and new viewpoints on matters of great significance. Further, teachers can protect students into challenging yet affirming dialogic experiences of internal conflict between views. In doing so, students are placed in powerful positions from which they can critique their previous views and forge new ones that they can carry into action.

As a teacher, I have come to realize the awe-ful power that we have to enter into deep and significant conversations with students that change the ethical ways they view the world and themselves. I continue to learn how we can extend the circle of care and the web of relationships in the classroom as we interact with students.

Some students have healthy, vibrant dynamic interactions with their peers, the world, and with themselves. Other students are less open to dissenting opinions and dissonant voices. However, all students have many more voices to share than the ones they first show us—including more ethical ones.

Ethical selves can be chosen, forged, and burnished in drama—not static individual selves, but dynamic relational selves that acknowledge and embrace internal contradictions in their views. Bakhtin imagines the self as "not a particular voice within, but a particular way of combining many voices within" (Morson and Emerson 1990, 213). For him the self is "a conversation, often a struggle, of discrepant voices with each other, voices (and words) speaking from different positions and invested with different degrees and kinds of authority" (Morson and Emerson 1990, 218).

In drama, students can explore and encounter multiple voices. As teachers, we can assist our students to choose themselves as ethical characters when we deepen and extend the conversations they have with each other, with us, and with themselves.

NOTES

1. Mimi Chenfeld is an inspiring teacher who has written several books and many articles on teaching. See especially Chenfeld 1983, 1987, and 1993. This quote comes from a personal conversation.

2. For a discussion of conflict in drama see my 1994 article. Conflict in plays is most often between characters. Teachers who think they are being "dramatic" when they pitch one student's views against another's miss the point that conflict is always experienced internally by the audience in the theatre. In the classroom, it is only when students internally experience conflicting points of view that drama exists.

3. Gavin Bolton, one of the foremost practitioners and theorists of drama, believes that "change in understanding" is "the most significant learning directly attributable to drama" (1979, 45).

4. Jeff also noted how influential Neil Postman's recent book *The End of Education* has been for him.

5. I use the terms "morality" and "ethics" interchangeably. Philip Jackson in *The Practice of Teaching* (1986) has shown how there are moral messages and meanings in every classroom interaction and every teacher choice.

6. For an illuminating example, see Melanie Fine, *Habits of Mind*, 1955 p. 55. In a tolerant progressive classroom where students talked about current issues when

faced with strong tensions between positions over Israeli Jews, students and teacher became more entrenched in their own initial views.

7. The writings of Mikhail Bakhtin are central to the views of ethics explored in this chapter. See my 1995 chapter for a more detailed analysis of ethics and drama. Bakhtin's views are in contrast to mainstream ethical discourses based primarily in Kantian morality which rely on notions of abstract principles of justice and moral codes by which we attempt to live. Kohlberg's views on moral development drew on Piaget's stages of development and were grounded in mainstream discourses of ethics. Critiques of these positions, especially by Gilligan (1982), re-oriented away from sole attention to abstract principles of justice and toward specific contexts and the relationships between people. Bakhtin extends this critique further in arguing that we are only ethical when we act with attention to context and a widening sense of our relationships with others.

8. Shifting perspectives, rupturing, and redirecting the flow of the drama serves to heighten student awareness, to defamiliarize current understandings, to encourage deep thought, and to maintain high levels of engagement in the drama activities which are experienced as repeatedly challenging and fresh. This is true when any kind of discourse or discourse convention is "ruptured" or changed in mid-stream (Cazden, 1987; Lemke, 1982; Rabinowitz, 1987).

9. The books used included *Rethinking Columbus,* Jane Yolen's *Encounters* and Michael Dorris' *Morning Girl.*

10. The term discourse is used in different disciplines with a variety of meanings. I am not using it as a synonym for talk. I am primarily drawing on the writings of Mikhael Bakhtin and Michel Foucault. For an overview of Foucault's ideas see Rabinow 1984.

11. These drama activities were not an attempt to *represent* "the" Taino point of view or stereotype them as "Indians." Rather, in the drama the students drew imaginatively on their research in order to shift their perspective to how Tainos *might* have lived.

12. This idea is based on Bill Bigelow's account of his teaching in *Rethinking Columbus* (1991).

4

Drama and Curriculum:
It Takes Two to Integrate

Jeffrey D. Wilhelm

At first (when we started the design project with hypermedia), I thought "Oh No"
what is this stuff? . . . but now I think we could do this the whole year long. I mean,
this is what we should do in school, don't you think? . . . We're learning everything,
and it's all together at the same time so you don't even notice . . . and it's fun too!
— Trixie, 7th grade, excited by the near completion of a research
project that made use of drama

DRAMA IN A SUPPORTING ROLE

This book illustrates how drama can be used to structure inquiry using
imaginary frames that create purposes and audiences for students' work.
Although drama frames may be developed and maintained over days or
even weeks, in the following three chapters we show how drama can be
used more strategically for short periods of time.

This chapter explores uses of significant drama teaching and learning
techniques in student-centered design projects. I illustrate how drama can
be both a cohesive force to integrate curriculum and a method to support
teaching and learning in integrated ways. Further, I show how effective
drama strategies can be as teacher interventions to unclog or stimulate students' thinking as they pursue long-term projects. This is drama, not in a

starring role or as a central feature, but as a move in the teacher's repertoire that helps to integrate, reframe, and extend learning at a point of need.

This story also marks my growing independence as a teacher who began to adapt, devise, and use drama as a natural part of my teaching. The actual drama work in the previous chapters was either designed by Brian, or by me with feedback from Brian. But in this chapter I describe how I struck out on my own and saw the opportunity to use drama methods and strategies during thematic units of instruction that emphasized the learning of significant academic content.

Drama had quickly become a natural, powerful and highly enjoyable part of my teaching and learning that was easily adapted by both me and my students. Brian and I both hope that this book provides readers with the motivation, models, and guidance that Brian gave to me, and that the book will therefore help you to reach the point that I describe here, practicing drama strategies as flexible techniques that can be used both spontaneously and through planning to aid student learning.

My team-teaching partner Paul Friedemann and I, over several years of team-teaching, adopted notions of learning-as-design and of theme-based teaching as powerful models for achieving significant, highly relevant, problem-cored, and student-centered integrated learning. This kind of learning has been at the core of progressive education in the elementary school and has long been espoused by middle school reformers (Beane 1975, 1980, 1990; Lounsbury and Vars 1978) and more recently by secondary school thinkers (e.g., NASSP, 1996). In this context, I discovered that drama works well as one of many teaching techniques that serve progressive education's curricular goals.

"Learning as design" centers on learning around problems the solutions to which require the construction of new understandings, for example, the design of knowledge. This is because the design model focuses on situated learning as it happens in real life. It is clear that real-life learning (Cf. Brown, Collins and DuGuid 1989) makes seamless and integrated use of knowledge from domains that we define as science, math, history, language arts, and the fine arts; in school, however, we persist in artificially separating learning into "subject areas." Beane (1990) writes that

> The subject approach presents numerous problems to schools in general . . . To begin with, it suggests a distorted view of real life as it is commonly experienced by people, including the young and probably most academicians when they are off-campus. Life and learning consist of a continuous flow of experiences around situations that require problem-solving in both large and small ways. When we encounter life situations or problems we do not ask,

'which part is science, which is mathematics, which is history, and so on?'
Rather we use whatever information or skills the situation itself calls for and
we integrate these in problem-solving . . . in real life the problem itself is at
the center and the information and skills are defined around the problem. In
other words, the subject approach is alien to life itself. Put simply, it is "bad"
learning theory (p. 45).

Why does the archaic organization of subject divisions in schools persist in the face of research, theory, and calls for reform that all insist that
this way of organizing education should be replaced with integrated,
problem-centered curricula? I have heard Ken Zeichner blame "the sa-
lience of the traditional"—the inability of schools to overcome the inertia of tradition as they attempt to enact new visions. John Lounsbury, in
conversation, related that integrated curriculum is so foreign to our traditional practices and notions that we "prefer to believe what we prefer to
be true"—that preference being those impoverished practices with which
we are more familiar. Beane (1993) blames outmoded historical concepts
such as classical humanism and faculty psychology that still organize curricula although no longer credited, and the university elite who insist that
the school curriculum look like that of the university. Whatever the reason, curriculum in practice remains true to its Latinate root meaning of a
"pre-set racecourse" that we require students to run around. My friend
Erv Barnes proposes that we need a new metaphor of curriculum as a
path and journey. In drama our journeys are always personal and they are
always social as well. In drama, students and teachers take journeys together—exploring the curriculum through shared imaginary experiences.
Though each student has individial experiences, students' paths cross and,
as Brian notes in Chapter 3, they also share common routes, campgrounds, and vistas.

Curriculum as a shared journey is a metaphor that fits nicely with
Beane's call for curriculum to be significant to students as it helps them
make sense of the world and their own lives. Beane further argues that curriculum should be general and practical in order to develop a wide variety
of learning processes that will allow for choice and growth in any direction;
should develop personal and social meanings; respect the dignity of students as capable and caring; be firmly grounded in democracy; honor diversity; be lifelike and lively; of great personal and social significance; and
should enhance seminal knowledge and skill development for all students
by providing clear contexts and purposes for writing, reading, learning, and
problem-solving. Beane argues that such a curriculum must be created by
teachers and students working together, must be integrated and holistic,

and must be centered around problems of interest and importance to both students and to society (1993, 17–22).

On rare occasions when true integrated learning has been implemented and studied, it has been found that nonsubject–oriented instruction has held many substantial advantages for students (*see* Vars 1992). The famous *Eight Year Study*, published in 1942 (Aiken), demonstrated that graduates from thirty high schools with experimental curricula outperformed their peers in traditional programs on both academic and social measures. It seems that even the claims that subject-matter orientation is important for college preparation are so flimsy as to be untenable.

Beane (1990), Lounsbury (1996), Brazee (1995), and other curriculum theorists suggest in various ways that part of the difficulty in achieving an authentic integrative curriculum is teachers' lack of familiarity with integrated curricula and practices, including a repertoire of teaching techniques that work towards integration. What teachers and students need, then, are processes for exploring, expressing, presenting, and re-presenting what we are coming to know; processes that open our hearts and minds to new ways of knowing and being. We propose drama as just such a technique. Drama is much more real, as we have seen, and much more closely linked to reality, and much more supportive of meaning-construction than most anything else we do in traditional, recitation-dominated schooling.

Curriculum is, Beane tells us, the totality of what we do in school, which includes the institutional features of schools and the processes that we use to learn. Drama is therefore a curriculum process that can organize integrated instruction. Drama provides a variety of techniques to engage all students and to orchestrate multifarious activities into a coherent whole. Students in drama sometimes work in pairs or in small groups, always returning to the whole group to report or to create a larger drama, sometimes working as audience and advisors to other small groups. Once students learn strategies like carousel or tableaux, these become tools they use with great facility when directed to do so by the teacher, or on their own for independent purposes. Once students know the basic systems of drama, they can use these systems to learn independently and cooperatively as the need arises.

At this point, drama becomes a mode of thought that can be manipulated in imagination to both experience and pursue solutions to practical problems. This is because drama helps us to create mental models that can be manipulated (*see* Chapter 3 for examples of how this is done in history and Chapter 6 for examples of how this is done in science). Drama provides a human crucible—a place to experiment with various meanings and possibilities. As such, drama is intimately connected to inquiry, an idea that we will explore in depth in the next chapter, an idea which is clearly tied up with the concept of integrated curricula.

DRAMA DELIVERS INTEGRATION!

Why is drama such an excellent match for use in an integrated curriculum? Drama, as Beane (1993) suggests schooling must, begins with the life and concerns lived by students at the point at which these intersect with important social concerns such as those we have or will see at play in past and future chapters: the nature of our own prejudice, the promise and responsibility of democracy, the nature of social ills like joblessness and welfare. These issues are presented respectfully and in great complexity. Simplistic answers like overcoming prejudice by force (*see* Chapter 5) or accepting a space trade (*see* Chapter 3) are confronted with human consequences and complexity. Drama is adaptable; it meets students in their current state of being and asks them to become more.

One problem with subject-oriented curriculum is that it focuses on information instead of on meaning, and on methods of learning instead of on reasons to learn. In drama, however, the methods are always wrapped up with and responsive to the reasons for learning that initiated the dramatic action. Yes—the engineering and metaphysics of learning are integrated in drama. Information is learned in the service of meeting human purposes, doing work, and solving problems.

Drama is problem centered, experiential, and holistic. It highlights the agency and meaning-making function of the learner. Drama is an antidote to the belief that cognition and affect, thought and feeling can and should be separated. This is because thinking, experimentation, self-perception, ethics (*see* Chapter 3), and feelings (*see* Chapter 2) are always part of drama. Moreover, drama is a form of student-centered inquiry (*see* Chapter 5) that explores profound questions and makes use of and enlivens primary sources. Drama makes the abstract accessible and concrete. The distant time of medieval castles is brought nearer; the nature of an animal's love for his master is made more real.

Drama offers teachers the chance for individual contact with students, so necessary both to responsive teaching and to an authentic, naturalistic assessment of learning. This kind of individual contact and interaction does not occur in traditional, whole group instruction. Drama lets kids act on their proclivity to interact. Many behaviors, like the desire to interact with peers, are perceived as disruptive in traditional classrooms but are of great use during drama work. In drama group work, everyone can be engaged, talking and creating meanings at the same time. The amount of student talk is exponentially increased because drama structures and focuses problem-centered peer exchanges. Forman and Cazden (1985, 330) summarize several studies showing "that peer interaction helps individuals acknowledge and integrate a variety of perspectives on a problem, and that this process of coordination, in turn, produces superior intellectual results." As we discussed in Chapter 2, all-important intersubjectivity is built from shared work. What one cannot do and know alone, one *can* do and know with the help of others. Drama always emphasizes the exploration and development of meaning with others.

Drama requires the achievement of understanding; the testing, applying, and acting out of a coherent schema of knowledge (*see* the section on the creation of the Columbus exhibit in Chapter 3). Above all, drama requires a reformed relationship of teachers and students. This leads to a more democratic, responsive, and effective kind of education that helps students to outgrow their current selves by assisting them to do what they cannot do alone.

I should like now to make one additional, slightly different point about the importance of collaboration and integration, and about the role of drama in helping these things happen. Drama provides an integrated context for various collaborative skills to be used as tools. The basic argument of Vygotskian educational theorists is that schools must work "to free the symbol systems of reading, writing, mathematics and science for use as tools . . . " so that they can be used to solve problems, do real-world work, and be used for thinking in new situations. "This conception is also consistent with an emerging consensus in cognitive psychology and education that language development, reading, writing and thinking are profoundly interconnected, and so *must be their instructional programs*" (Tharp and Gallimore 1988, 108, the italics are mine). And if this is not enough of an argument for using drama in an integrated curriculum, read on. Vogt (1985) found the most powerful and productive activity setting for guiding learning and for assisting more expert performances was that of project collaboration—pursuing projects in which participants worked together as designers of something new.

So perhaps we should think of drama not only as a collaborative method of teaching in integrated settings, but also as a way of bringing about powerful and holistic curricular experiences. Another use of drama is that humans often act their ways into new ways of being and understanding. Guskey (1986) found that changes in teaching practices preceded changes in teachers' attitudes and beliefs. Michael Fullan and other reformers (Fullan and Pomfret 1977; Rosenholtz 1986) have also found that when teachers work in teams to collaboratively shape curricula and determine the values to be embodied in those curricula (whether on their own or with their students) their educational attitudes, philosophies and practices will change. "Because of the powerful intersubjectivities developed during the joint productive activity of the project team, cognition and motivation themselves are transformed" (Tharp and Gallimore 1988, 210). You see, group projects on real problems of great significance bring about changes in understanding *and* practice for adults as well as kids. Collaborative, holistic learning situations work to support learning and changed ways of being in the world.

LEARNING AS DESIGN

Paul and I adapted Beane's proposal (1990, 1993) that teachers and students work together to identify themes of interest and importance. Within these themes (Beane suggests themes like identities, wellness, independence, and many others; our themes were basically chosen for us by our district's curricula), students identify issues, problems, and questions they want to explore as a class and in smaller groups. These groups can then pursue inquiry and teach each other what they have learned, providing different angles on a theme. As students engage in their learning, they make use of general skills and learning processes involving thinking, feeling, problem-solving, making ethical decisions, self-concepting, and self-esteeming. They search for completeness and meaning and use what they learn as a basis for social action.

The metaphor of "learning as design" is one way to approach theme-based learning. This approach specifies the actual learning processes to be used. The notion of design harkens back to Dewey's (1910) progressive education and his commitment to learner-centered and teacher-guided approaches. The idea is for students to develop rather than receive knowledge, and it recasts the metaphor for teaching from information transmission to one of knowledge construction. Accordingly, Perkins (1986) argues that we should recast learning as a process of design. Through the design process, students experience knowledge as a human creation that is a response to human needs and problems. This knowledge will necessarily have a situation-specific function and structure and will be revised as new problems, situations, information, and viewpoints arise. In my own design-oriented teaching, I used drama to advantage to reinforce all these points as I framed instructional situations.

Over the past several years, Paul and I have used various design environments that involved creating books and instructional materials for peers or younger students, designing hypermedia and video documentaries or other kinds of resources for local libraries or the school's cable station, putting together and participating in exhibits for museums or living history fairs, making models, or implementing community service programs. In our classroom, drama often played a part in the creation or presentation of these design products. On occasion, students have scripted and performed their own formal theater presentations, in which case drama itself became a design artifact.

The model of design is very similar to traditional project-based learning, but with these differences: the design approach is more concerned with the authenticity and correctness of the material (which is why the teacher must be involved and ready to intervene, challenge, and guide student learning), and with the systematicity, extensibility, and usability of the knowledge artifacts that students design.

For example, projects often show students' responses to curricular materials, but do not necessarily accurately reflect our most current human understandings of various phenomena. Projects often provide a single example of student activity, whereas design focuses on the creation of a system of patterned understandings. In design, students are encouraged to create various representations of a single idea (*Cf.* Brian's use of Bakhtin's insistence on knowledge's being constructed in the interactions among multiple perspectives), to consider the contextual importance of ideas, and to think about and express relationships among ideas. Janvier (1987) has found that multiple and linked representations of ideas provide the cornerstone of true understanding, because students will then see how ideas are situated and what kind of work these ideas can do. This is a far cry from the limited understanding students take from lectures and recitation style classes, and even what they take away from unguided projects. We know that in real learning communities, models are tested, critiqued, modified, and extended by the community. Even when projects are "one-shot" propositions, design artifacts are built so that others can revise and add to them. Finally, though projects are often displayed to wider audiences, they are rarely used. Design projects are made to be used by various audiences for a variety of human purposes.

When students become actively involved in drama, or in any other environment in which they are engaged in building deep understandings of complex phenomena, teachers must adopt a style of teaching Sheingold (1991) calls "adventurous teaching" (Carver, Lehrer, Connell and Erickson 1992). These authors continue: "Such teaching involves a radical shift toward coaching individuals or guiding small groups working co-operatively on varied tasks suited to their own interests and abilities, yet related to the primary concepts being studied" (p. 386). In such learning, the students are regarded as apprentices to the teacher, who must be ready to orchestrate activities and raise the level of purpose at any time to push them toward more complex understandings. The teacher may use a variety of techniques to challenge and extend the learner, including, in my case, the use of drama.

My friend Rich Lehrer (1991, 1993) has carefully specified the kinds of skills involved in the process of design: students must integrate and orchestrate a whole complex of skills as they go through a recursive process of asking questions, decomposing problems, collaborating to manage the design project, finding information, developing information (e.g., through interviews, surveys, drama), selecting and analyzing information, organizing information, representing information, evaluating the design through feedback, revising, and presenting the product. (For a fuller discussion and examples of the design process and illustrations of its use with hypermedia, see Wilhelm 1995; Wilhelm and Friedemann 1998).

When Paul and I first were made familiar with this approach through our work with Lehrer and Erickson, Paul exclaimed, "Hey, this is everything worth teaching right here! This could be the whole curriculum, K to 12!" He made these comments more than once, and they echo those made by Trixie (quoted at the beginning of this chapter) when she was completing a design project two years later.

Two examples of design: Instead of memorizing facts about animal adaptations, students would design an animal that could thrive on the prairies. This process of design necessitates asking questions, learning a wide variety of complex information regarding environments and animal adaptation, *and* applying this knowledge through the use of design skills to create a product that displays understanding. Instead of merely identifying body parts, students can be asked to design a joint or a purification system. In our own classes, our most significant projects saw students creating extensive hypermedia and video documents to teach various audiences about questions important both to the students and their intended audience.

One can clearly see how design and drama-based learning are both aligned with responsive and constructivist teaching, but set against traditional forms of passive and receptive learning. Teachers operate on "the crest of the future's breaking wave" or on "the knife edge," as Paul and I used to joke. At the point of need, we would model skills, teach minilessons, ask leading questions, provide cognitive structuring and continuous alternative assessments, and make use of design tools like hypermedia that supported the creation of multiple representations and links between bits of information. Drama strategies were often integral to our teaching moves.

One can also see how such learning and teaching are necessarily integrated, as teachers and students bring to bear any information and skills necessary to solving the problems of design that are currently at hand.

DRAMA AND DESIGN: A CULTURAL JOURNALISM UNIT

One of the topics required by our middle school curricula was the study of culture. Paul and I decided to use this topic as a "theme" that would help us to teach other curricular objectives from various subjects in an integrated fashion. For instance, our various curricula called for the teaching of outlining, myths and fables, the metric system, conversions, study skills, oral presentations, and a variety of other content and skills that a design project could purposefully contextualize.

During the project, which lasted approximately ten weeks of language-arts and social studies lessons in blocked-out time periods, groups of students identified a culture, asked questions of interest, and researched those questions through a variety of required means: reading of various materials, electronic research, contacts with cultural agencies, interviews with cultural informants, studying artifacts, and the like. They then created hypermedia documents that posed their questions and set out the answers they had found. (Note: Hypermedia is a computer platform in which information is entered onto "cards" or "screens" that can be linked to various other cards in a variety of ways through the use of "buttons." The information on any particular card can include text, pictures, drawings, graphics, sound and video clips—hence the term "hyper media." The two differences between hypertext and traditional text is its multimedia format and its non linearity, that is, cards need not be read in any particular order but rather can be linked in any way the author anticipates will meet readers' needs.)

Although we felt that our culture unit was very successful through its first few years, we also felt that many of the final hypermedia documents lacked focus, a sense of audience, and a certain degree of specificity and vitality. It was then that I decided to use drama as a way of framing the project and of intervening to cognitively structure a sense of audience, purpose, and challenge into the design process.

To start the unit, I used drama over short time periods to highlight the notion of culture. In each drama, I framed the students as people who had reasons to be interested in "our" culture—each frame provided the students with ironic, dialogic, and often very amusing cultural perspectives. Each such perspective also gave the students' new lenses to distance themselves from their "own" culture and to see it with new eyes.

With different classes, I did short versions of the Columbus drama (*see* Chapter 3), asking groups of students to imagine they were Taino Indians who had found a lost child. What would this child need to learn to become one of us? How would we talk about religion, education, government and other cultural institutions when we went to Columbus to make the case that we represented a culture equal to his own?

In other classes, we created a drama where we discovered a colony of Yeti in the mountains and attempted to acculturate these beings into our human society. As we did so, we asked the Yeti to accompany us to school, to operate a mailbox, and a soda vending machine. In role as Yetis, we created our own culture and compared aspects of it, such as our government—for example, talking in a circle until consensus was reached with all members—with the U.S. style of governance by delegating authority to central figures through elections. In other cases, we used excerpts of stories from aboriginal Australia such as *Walkabout* and *Songlines* to create dramatic sequences that displayed differences in culture. A funny excerpt from an anthropological parody—"Body Ritual Among the Nacerima," ("American" spelled backwards) was used to highlight how people from other cultures might respond to and classify our own cultural behavior. In this parody, bathrooms are identified as "shrines" in which body rituals take place. "The focal point of the shrine is a box or chest which is built into the wall. In this chest are kept the many charms and magical potions without which no native believes he could live. . ." and so on (Miner 1956, 504).

In this same spirit, students engaged in a drama in which they played associates of the alien Professor Xargle (from the Professor Xargle books by Jeanne Willis) studying U.S. teenage subcultures. In role, students identified aspects of culture and their importance to how American teens live and think.

These sessions involved hilarious results. When a group of boys were observing "pre-preliminary mating rituals among middle school humanoids at body movement festivals (dances)" they noted a variety of "female non-availability signs" including, but not limited to, the wearing of a ring, the repeated statement "I have to leave to babysit," sniffing of the nose and other allergic reactions at the approach of "an unsuitable body movement partner," and the seemingly permanent attachment inside a circle of other females or to the arm of another boy. This group of Xargle's apprentices could discern a variety of "cultural pre-preliminary mating rites" but could not "understand the principles by which the humanoid females use these rites." They wrote that these rites were probably a way of preparing the young to make sensible mating choices later in life, but doubted their efficacy. One boy, Mark, wrote that, "Humanoid adults would be better off to choose the mates of their young as we do, based on compatibility factors such as intelligence and interests. When left to choose on their own, humanoids attach too much importance to aspects such as physical attractiveness, which quickly change to fatness once marriage is achieved."

These boys obviously had their own axe to grind but they had fun doing it. In this way, in a few short sessions, students were helped to experience and to think about the notions of culture and cultural difference and to consider how and why culture is developed and expressed.

After an average of three drama sessions, students were engaged in a discussion about culture. Small groups in roles as Xarglites were asked "What are the various aspects of culture? What different kinds of human cultures are there and why? Why do humans need to know about culture? In what situations might humans need a deep knowledge of another culture?" After students reported and discussed their findings at a Xarglite symposium, we left the drama world. At this point, students had usually indicated some preliminary understanding of culture and had developed some reasons for learning about it. At this point we asked students to identify an actual human culture or subculture of interest and to begin developing preliminary questions of interest about the culture.

After questions were asked, we worked to frame the design work as a kind of modified mantle of the expert drama (Heathcote and Bolton 1995)(1). When the questions were shared and critiqued for their research value (*see* Wilhelm and Friedemann 1998), students were also asked who else might want to know the answers to these questions. Depending on their queries, groups came up with different answers—and different potential frames for further drama work—such as trade delegations, groups from the United Nations (e.g., security forces, humanitarian aid, or literacy developers), missionaries, travelers, business people, or political operatives such as spies, and even exchange students.

Often, a discussion ensued about how to differentiate countries from cultures, and how the idea of culture was often mapped onto the boundaries of a country. Even though many groups chose cultural groups such as the Ojibway, Zulu, or Bedouin, most students chose a group determined by political nationality, such as Germans or Japanese. We took care that students differentiated between culture and country.

Students always had an awareness of audience: a future audience of peers but also often audiences within a drama world. Students knew that they would ultimately share their hypermedia projects with their peers, their third-grade learning buddies, and with the public during a Learning Fair. We also sometimes shared documents with a partner school or made them available in electronic form or at the public library. In addition to these general audiences, we asked the students to imagine a specific real-world audience that might use their document. Mark's group, for instance, chose travelers and exchange students to be the audience of their document on Italy. Trixie's Scotland group chose a trade delegation of area businessmen and farmers to be the audience of their hypermedia project.

Students then were asked what role they should play—in other words, what agencies or businesses handled their kinds of questions for the audiences they had identified? Mark's group became a tour company; Trixie's partners decided to be an agency of business consultants specializing in export.

At this point, questions were refined and research begun. Early on in the research, I tried to use drama strategies with each group to help focus their research. I called these strategies *scene-setting* and *problem-scenarios*.

For example, Mark was busy working on research about the Italian economy. His partners, true to their purpose of creating a hypermedia document to familiarize long-term visitors with Italian culture, were busy preparing substacks to answer questions such as Casey's: "What is Italian family life like?" To set her up, we conducted a short role play, in which I, as a future exchange student, voiced my concerns about my dietary restrictions and about table manners. How would I interact at dinner? Would I be expected to help cook or clean up? Would my dietary needs be met? This brief role play helped to focus Casey's research.

While researching her question, she had learned the jobs family members do during mealtimes. She learned how to make spaghetti and lasagna noodles from scratch and made recipe cards. She learned the slang names for twelve different kinds of noodles (e.g. rotini: sewer pipes). She learned that the father sits at the head of the table and gets to eat out of the big pasta bowl after everyone else has been served . Why? Because the bowl will have the most sauce, which father deserves. This discovery had led her to design some special cards for female travelers and exchange students regarding sex roles in Italy and "attitudes towards women." Back to her original topic, she discovered there are several different kinds of Italian cuisine and learned what kind of wine or gift to bring when invited to dinner in different parts of Italy. She was surprised by the culture of gift-giving in Italy.

Meanwhile, Mark was in trouble. His research had been guided by his question: How does the Italian economy work? His research centered on major Italian industries. His initial issue tree, designed to organize what he had learned and to suggest ways of dividing information onto different hypercards, was a total mess. He included "Major Industries" as a subtopic of "Free Market Economy." As subtopics of "Major Industries," he had listed items like "the lire" and "money system." How is "money system" an example of an "industry," I asked him. "I'm just trying to answer my question!" he answered in frustration.

Time for drama.

Mark played the role of travel consultant, and I played the role of a tourist leaving for a six-month stay in Italy. "OK, Mark," I said to start us off, "What do you have for me? What do I need to know about the Italian economy?" He began to talk about the lire, referring to his notes. "How much are they worth in dollars?" I asked him. "Does the exchange rate change much? Should I buy lire now for the whole trip, or should I keep dollars and exchange them as I need money?" He didn't know. "OK, Mark. I'm headed to Venice, Florence, San Gimigiano, and Rome, then on to Sicily. How expensive are these places? Where should I stay longest if I get short on money? Can I use credit cards in these places? How will they figure the exchange rate if I do so?"

We switched it around, with his playing the role of an Italian exchange student. What questions did he have about the American economy?

After these short role plays, Mark went to several classmates and asked what they would want to know about the Italian economy as visitors there. They listed several questions: What kind of jobs do people have? What do they do with their money? What happens if you don't have a job? How are prices for things different here in the United States? What affects earning and spending power in Italy?

Mark's resulting plan for a hyperstack on money had conversion tables on exchange rates, suggestions regarding the cost of living in various places, and ideas on cheap places to stay and eat and on ways to travel. His stack on jobs had cards about the fashion industry, making race cars, wine-tasting, and the influence of the Mafia on business. He made suggestions about things to purchase while in Italy, and fashion houses and car show-rooms to visit. "This was a lot more fun than what I was going to do," he admitted. "And a lot more fun to read," I added.

Trixie, before beginning the actual design of her hypercards, had organized her information about the climate and natural resources of Scotland into a beautiful issue tree. In role as a businessman, I asked her, "How does the climate affect the agriculture and industry?" After she deftly answered this question, I asked her, "How does this inform the two of us about the kinds of goods they might want from us?" A lively discussion ensued during which I asked her about money and metric conversions, if we needed to translate bushels into metric tons, what I could reasonably charge for wheat and other products. We wondered aloud about whether the Scots would be susceptible to coffee bars, or whether they were too enamored of tea. Trixie promised to find out. She later interviewed a couple from town who had just returned from Scotland, and—through a local contact—was able to talk to a member of the Chicago Board of Trade about international grain deals. I can honestly say that she learned more about this than I had ever hoped to understand.

Afterwards, Trixie added to her issue tree by showing how she would link information about climate to her cards on agriculture, and link her cards on Scottish products to cards of information outlining Scottish imports and possible import niches for American goods. These became crosslinked connections between her hypercard substacks after her hypermedia document was completed.

One requirement during the research process was for students to read several cultural tales to try to make a connection between one of the tales and one of their group's driving questions. They were to share this tale and what they felt it contributed to their cultural understanding through the use of symbolic story representations. Mark read several Italian tales that he felt had a similar theme. Because the tales were short, he performed *symbolic story representations* (*see* Chapter 2) of two of them, "Crab" and "The Thoughtless Abbot." In each, a peasant is able to befriend and help a more powerful noble personage through sheer gall and guesswork, thereby earning friendship and fortune. Mark used a die to symbolize the central focus of both, which he thought was "take risks and trust your smarts." His peers added that both heroes had a good dose of luck. Mark retorted that Italians made their own luck, by "putting themselves in the game, man, and trying things. It may make things crazy, but when things work! Wow!" He thought the stories related to the innovative nature of much of Italy's industry. "Their culture is about passion—they don't hold back—they try things—they're on the cutting edge, man!" he informed his group. This became a theme of his hyperstack.

Drama played a supporting role at two other points in the design project. When peers responded to first drafts of the hypermedia documents, these peers were asked to take on the role of a client interested in using the document as a resource. Mark was reviewing the project from a group who had worked on the dual culture of Rwanda. The ethnic split in that country had started a terrible civil war during the time that we were working on the unit. We had suggested to the students studying Rwanda that they attempt to explore and explain this conflict in their document. Although this led them in a slightly different direction than they had originally intended, the chance to follow the conflict in the news interested them. Therefore, Mark and the other reviewers of their document were framed as United Nations peacekeepers being briefed on the situation.

From this role, they asked many intelligent questions about the nature of the Hutu and Tutsi, the traditional nature of their relationship, about other countries in which these tribal groups lived and the political climate in those, and how this conflict compared with the war in Bosnia. Although the Rwanda group could not answer all these questions, this did lead them to seek answers, and thus to create a more polished final product. As a sidenote, I have often observed students respond to and ask questions of each others' work. Usually they have little to say without some kind of structure and purpose. When response is structured by drama, I have often observed and kept journal notes about the increased number and improved quality of the questions.

Finally, when the students made formal presentations of their final documents, some groups were asked to do so in role. Trixie took on the role of business consultant and dressed in a blazer for her presentation. The actual document made use of dramatic elements by simulating a tour of Scottish industry and agriculture. Each card was another stop on the tour, and the audience and their anticipated questions were addressed.

SEEING THE CONNECTIONS

In Chapter 6, there are more examples of how drama can be used in a supporting role to integrate content area instruction and to help students solve problems by focusing their attention, making the abstract concrete, and foregrounding the human concerns involved in their work with science and math.

In the unit just described, drama was initially used to access existing knowledge of a culture and to generate new insights and background experiences that could inform their work. Drama roles were also used in initial tasks that built commitment to the project and provided a focus and audience for their work. This dramatic framing of the project helped students to see the connections between their project and real world concerns. Drama used during minilessons helped students to see that they needed to do more research, hone skills, or revise their thinking by emphasizing that the project was not about learning information or skills only, but about learning so that they could do things. Drama helped students to see that math- and science-based problems, like converting money and explaining the effects of climate on agriculture, needed to be included in their documents. Drama helped students ask questions, organize information, and even represent it using computer technology.

Framing the work with drama helped students to see that what they were doing was telling a kind of story; this helped them organize their information and provided a framework for their learning. Drama enhanced the students' understanding of the human dimensions of their work. The strategic use of drama helped in the ultimate integration: that of learning and life. We see once again that drama is not about reenactment, but about the collaborative building of new understandings and the telling of new stories.

O'Neill and Lambert (1982) write about this ultimate synthesis and integration: "drama offers the possibility of a synthesis between language, feeling and thought, which can enrich the individual's inner world and increase his or her awareness and understanding of the outer world, as well as his or her competence and confidence in operating within it. It would be prodigal of the drama teacher to neglect such possibilities" (p. 20). Amen.

NOTES

1. Our work was similar to mantle of the expert in that students were cast as experts with a problem and were helped through drama to internalize the expertise of their role. It was different in that much of our work was not done inside a specified drama world. Other similarities and differences existed as well.

5

Drama as Inquiry: Students and Teachers as Coresearchers[1]

Brian Edmiston

Doing research with drama helped us to really understand things and to make sure we understand. [When] we didn't know what to do in the drama, we knew we didn't know enough. Somehow it was pretty hard to fake because you have to do something . . . . if you do something and you don't feel it or it doesn't seem right, you go back and learn more and do it again. You know, like you always say about "research"— go back and "resee" it.

—Ned, grade 7

[The drama] kind of brought doubt. My original opinion kind of went down, then up again with some doubt. I had different reasons for my opinions, like the effect on the Vietnamese people which I'd never thought about — how they got killed and their houses destroyed and stuff . . . so in a way, my opinion is stronger, but it's less sure. I'm kind of more open to that there are other opinions that are strong and stuff even though you might disagree [with those other opinions].

—Ron, grade 7

"How could someone end up shooting a machine gun at rival gang members in the St. Valentine's Day Massacre planned by Al Capone's gang?" "What did Hank Aaron have to do off the ballfield to become great?"

"How did the Great Depression affect ordinary people's lives?" "What would be the effects of suffering through the Holocaust?" These were some of the research questions that Jeff and I explored with his students in May 1995 when Jeff once again invited me into the school to help students with their projects.

The students had spent three weeks working on final inquiry projects from the integrated unit on the theme of Civil Rights and Social Issues discussed in Chapter 3. Consistent with the idea of a problem- and project-centered curriculum, small groups of students had chosen to pursue some personally meaningful inquiries related to the theme. Many had voluntarily begun to use drama strategies, which Jeff and I had previously introduced to them.

In previous chapters, we have shown the power of drama: to introduce and extend students' involvement in units of inquiry, to integrate the curriculum, and to engage students in reading and other essential learning processes.

This chapter illuminates how, in conjunction with other methodologies, drama can become a significant mode for conducting research in small groups where students (and for a time, teachers,) are co-researchers (2). Drama can be used both as a method when students work alone or with a teacher in the exploration of research questions and also by students in the presentation of the results of inquiry.

As teachers, Jeff and I used drama strategically with small groups for short periods (one or two forty-minute sessions) to help students pursue their research purposes and to create spaces in which students could move beyond their current understandings through zones of proximal development. Drama, as we have seen, emphasizes meaning making through interaction, imagined experiences in multiple contexts, reflection, exploration, discovery, making connections, seeing implications, and the implementation and use of new understandings beyond the drama worlds. But deeper learning will occur and more complex understandings will develop if students interact in contexts in which, in dialogue, there is a sharing of expertise, a respectful challenge to superficial ideas, and an intermingling of different perspectives. This happens in peer groups that work together productively—it also occurs most effectively when teachers work with small groups of students to focus on their particular questions, understandings, misconceptions, and viewpoints.

DRAMA AND RESEARCH

Each group of two to four students in Jeff's five classes had chosen a topic and conducted extensive library research. They had gathered factual information and read applicable books; many had read relevant literature, interviewed informants, or watched videos about their topic. In addition, many groups had begun to incorporate drama strategies into their work. The unit's outcome, which had been agreed on with the students, was for each group to create a video documentary to inform their classmates and inspire some kind of social action or transformed thinking about the issue they were researching (3).

As many of the students wrote first drafts of their video scripts, they indicated dissatisfaction with their questions, understandings, findings, or how they were approaching their topics. When Jeff told his classes that I was interested in working through drama with groups to help them explore their topics in more depth, many students wanted to work with me and/or with Jeff. Over the course of the following week, thirty students in nine different groups used drama as a research tool. I conducted most of the initial sessions, and Jeff conducted follow-up sessions and student interviews.

What is Research?

Inquiry is another name for research which, according to Webster's 9th New Collegiate Dictionary, means "careful or diligent search, inquiry or investigation." From the first five minutes I spent with two of Jeff's students who were researching the Mafia during the 1920s, as I heard them talk about books they had consulted and saw their notebooks, it was clear that they had been carefully conducting inquiries.

For professionals, the "search" of research revolves around a key question or a series of questions that researchers clarify, and attempt to answer, as they pursue their inquiries into a particular topic. Jeff's students were similarly engaged in serious searches. These boys who were researching the Mafia wanted to know: "Who was Al Capone?" They had become clearer about factual details, historical events, and social aspects of the Mafia. Like all researchers they had collected and investigated "data." The students had consulted nearly all the relevant books in the school library that mentioned the Mafia, had collected photographs, and had read biographical accounts of mobsters. They had asked their parents about the topic but had had no success in finding "informants" (people who are considered important sources of information) to interview. Because they had not been alive in the 1930s, they could not make direct observations as many researchers do and although they would have liked to visit Chicago, such a trip was considered impractical. All Jeff's students had used the "methodology" of library research to gather data. These two boys were determining "results" of their study as they analyzed and interpreted the data they had gathered. They had some provisional answers to the question that had initiated their research: they knew about details like the St. Valentine's Day massacre and how the Mafia used extortion and ran "speakeasies." Like many researchers, they had found that in looking for answers they had come up with more questions. For example, in conversation with me they asked the question noted above: "How could someone end up shooting a machine gun at rival gang members in the St. Valentine's Day Massacre planned by Al Capone's gang?" Professional researchers ideally conduct their studies carefully and systematically: they "re-search" in the sense that they revisit questions and are cautious at every step to ensure that whatever results are presented are interpretations which can reasonably be drawn from an analysis of the data (4). These boys were more ready to rush to conclusions: they had concluded that anyone who really wanted to could have avoided getting caught up in the Mafia.

Elements of Research

Clearly, Jeff's students were following professional research models. Their inquiries had the core components of all research:

- questions
- researchers
- information/informants
- methodologies
- data
- results/interpretations

The students were coresearchers in their small groups as they pursued questions collaboratively, shared information, and critiqued each others' interpretations.

There are a host of ways—or methodologies—for conducting research in the classroom: reading; interviewing people; studying artifacts, documents, photographs; and watching documentaries. Drama is one research methodology, which can be used in conjunction with others, to gather and interpret data. When drama is used for inquiry, students gather data that are shared from memory, selected from books, presented as words and images, shaped with others, interpreted, and critiqued together. In drama, students can "re-search" when they revisit questions and reposition themselves to reconsider ideas and understandings as they re-look in different ways at the world they are studying together.

RESEARCHERS AND INFORMANTS

Professional researchers who ask questions about people's lives usually talk with informants in order to find out their relevant experiences, reflections, and understandings (5). Informants contextualize and amplify the information researchers find in books; they may also question positions, provide alternative views, and affect researchers' assumptions and inquiries (6). Drama used as an inquiry tool can have a similar effect on student researchers.

Student researchers who are interested in the same questions as professionals may have the opportunity to interview others, but most students will only read and talk *about* people, especially when they are separated from them in time and/or space. In drama, students can imagine the perspectives of informants (7).

The use of independent reading as the major method of gathering data may be problematic for many students, given Jeff's findings as outlined in Chapter 2. Gathering mountains of data will not necessarily bring the social worlds of other people alive for students. Looking at photographs and videos will help "resistant" readers construct images of another time and place, as will accompanying short factual or fictional first-person narratives of events. Reference books, which present abstract generalizations from a detached acultural point of view largely devoid of social contexts, may be barriers rather than windows into other times and places. Even "proficient" readers may experience texts as largely unconnected or disjointed threads of information, dialogue, and image (8).

Inquiry in Social Worlds

Student researchers must imagine social worlds if they want to go beyond the decontextualized facts and information of texts. To inquire into a topic in depth, they must be able to imaginatively amplify, extend, and reinterpret words and images and weave them into a cultural fabric to reveal patterns of human interactions, details of experiences, and create understandings of moments of significant action.

They must be able to go beyond dry facts and threadbare narratives; they need to be able to identify with more points of view than those from which stories are told. They must also learn how to read sources to make connections, and imagine details, events, times, places, people, and relationships from a variety of perspectives that are often inferred but not directly described in the accounts or stories they discover in the library. For example, to understand Al Capone, students needed to imagine from viewpoints of Al Capone's "family" as well as his victims; to recreate the Vietnam-era culture of protest, students had to discover why people protested *for* as well as against the war in Vietnam; and to avoid depersonalizing unemployed people during the Depression, students had to know something of the personal histories of people standing in never-ending breadlines.

Ideally, students' research questions send them to talk to informants who will assist them to see the world from their various points of view. Informants can raise new questions, reinterpret findings, and problematize simplistic approaches.

Because drama enables students to collaboratively create, enter into, and wonder about other social worlds, drama can be used as a tool for inquiry into the meanings of people's experiences in other times or places. In drama, students can imagine how a variety of informants might see the world and critique other views. In drama, students can adopt the stances of both researcher and informant (9).

Stances of Researcher and Informant

In drama, students may take up the perspectives of multiple "informants" as they imagine the experiences of people in the worlds of, for example, Chicago in the 1920s, protests against the Vietnam War in the 1960s, or the Great Depression of the 1930s. Yet, students may always critique and amplify their "findings" when they dialogue with those positions as "researchers."

Students can shift between the stances of researcher and informant. When drama is intentionally used as a tool for inquiry, students (assisted by the teacher) can become more purposeful about their shift from one posture to the other. The students already see themselves as researchers and thus have a clear reason to evaluate their experiences in drama.

The students shift between the stances of researchers and informants as the drama progresses. They will often do so without teacher intervention when they slip in and out of role, interact as if they were other people, or talk as themselves. However, if we are aware of the significance of switching between these postures, we can intervene at one moment in order to structure their interactions as various informants and at another moment to ask for their interpretations as researchers.

Jeff and I, as teachers, were coresearchers with the students. We also pursued the questions of their inquiries (10). As needed, we raised questions, provided information, and supported the students' plans. We also remained open to new ways of looking at each topic and in role adopted perspectives of informants in order to provide information, perspectives, and raise questions from *inside* the social worlds of the students' inquiries.

My work in forty minutes with the "Mafia group" illustrates how I adopted different informant perspectives and enabled the students to shift among the stances of researcher and various informants. The two boys wanted to find out how a person could have pulled the machine gun trigger but could not imagine how so "ordinary" a person could get so caught up in the Mafia that they could not have avoided involvement in the St. Valentine's Day massacre.

I structured the drama so that they would be both informants and reseachers by placing them in situations in which they adopted perspectives from which they imaginatively experienced the power of the Mafia to manipulate people into actions they would ordinarily have avoided—and then repeatedly asked the students-as-researchers how difficult it would have been to say "No" in such situations. I moved the students through a sequence of encounters from boys selling fruits and vegetables on a street corner from a handcart, through running a corner store that was operated as a front for storing alcohol, to Mafia members who had to prove their loyalty. I adopted the perspectives of fellow street vendor, F.B.I. agent, Mafia members at various levels of involvement, and family members. As the boys became more and more entangled in Mafia activities, first unwittingly, then to avoid being hurt, and finally to protect their families, as coresearcher I repeatedly returned to their research question. They became more critical of their initial position that people could have just said "No." The students wanted me to push them to the point at which the logic of picking up a machine gun made sense and was no longer seen as an impossibility. They experienced ways in which unscrupulous people can blackmail others into actions by promises and threats to themselves and their families.

Several times they tried to do the "right thing" and cooperate with or contact the police. However, as researchers, they began to problematize these actions; they recognized inherent dilemmas when I shifted to a Mafia position to imply and warn against fatal consequences for them or their families.

By the end of the session, as informants, the boys had created and interpreted a world of the Mafia and, as researchers, they had used drama to pursue a question as well as to reach and critique some conclusions. They said that now they could understand how a person might indeed fire a machine gun at others—they had gunned me down despite my cries for mercy. Pat remarked at the end of the session that previously as a reseacher, "I just didn't get it." Imagining the experiences of Mafia informants was very important for him. Pat had finally been able to see from a position "inside" a Mafia "family"—as he said, they had become members of "the family of hate."

Multiple Informant Stances

Taking up the perspectives of other positions during inquiry is critical for the development of multifaceted views and meanings. Students can then construct understandings as they dialogue with each other, with the teacher in and out of role, and with themselves about various informants' positions.

Buddy and Ron were researching the Vietnam War and noted how drama expanded their awareness. Buddy explained that "we got to see that there were other ways of looking at it [the war] . . . It helps you see other points of view that you can work from." Ron noted that "We were so many people. We were everywhere . . . I was inside so many different characters. . . protesters, army, politicians, parents [of soldiers], Vietnamese people." He reported that he had never really thought about what the Vietnamese people went through, until doing the drama. "That really changed me."

Students seem to adopt most easily points of view with which they have already identified. These may be the points of view that are already privileged in texts, for example, a narrator's point of view. The Underground Railroad group of four girls had read some slave narrratives and readily adopted the perspectives of enslaved people eager for news of Harriet Tubman. However, in drama we can *shift* point of view at will and imagine from multiple positions including those of people not mentioned directly in texts students have read. For example, these girls had only read about references to abolitionists, yet readily adopted their position in order to plan a response to the Fugitive Slave Act that made people subject to imprisonment if caught assisting runaway slaves.

Resisting Informants' Stances

Everyone, including researchers, resists identifying with some points of view; in doing so, we limit our potential for understanding. Researchers who interview others can try to hear from the different positions as they later reflect on transcripts; drama can similarly give voice to those whose views have been silenced.

In drama, students can begin to imagine the world from points of view which initially may seem peripheral to them or difficult to adopt. The Great Depression group began to understand more about being unemployed people in the 1930s. Maria recalled how significant the drama perspectives were for her. "After reading, finding the photographs, and even interviewing people I didn't get why people couldn't get jobs or money. [After the drama] I knew how it could happen, because I had a chance to be like people back then. I know now how people felt without jobs and how they helped each other cope."

Some potential perspectives may be difficult to adopt because they are painful for the students. Janne, one of the girls in the Underground Railroad group, noted the following soon after their drama session. "[The hardest part of the dramas] was when we had to pretend we had to leave older and weaker people behind, because we knew we would have to run . . . we didn't want the dogs to get them or for them to drown . . . so we didn't even tell them we were going and we knew we would never see them again. . . That was so hard . . . After we felt the dangers, what it would be like to run away, the risks, the excitement, being so afraid, being almost caught . . . we knew we made the right decision [not to bring the others] but our being happy at being free wasn't the same because they were still slaves and we wondered what had happened to them."

The perspectives of other informants may be resisted because a student initially disagrees with that way of seeing the world. In his Vietnam War research, Ron had adopted such a firm antiwar stance that he found it difficult to imagine why anyone would have wanted to join the military. However, Ron shows how significant it can be to have even a very brief perspective shift in drama. For no more than two minutes, he adopted the position of an army recruiter and was able to see from his point of view. After the drama, Ron reported that it "was hard [to imagine I was an army recruiter] because I was so much for the protesters." When he reflected on the perspective of the military recruiter he noted: "I felt like no one respected me . . . I saw how people hated hippies and how they had a point how the hippies were against what they really believed in and wouldn't listen and you could see them as lazy." Buddy also reconsidered protests for their effectiveness. He wrote that big protest demonstrations didn't "work" because, "there were beatings and fighting when we wanted peace . . . and when the antiwar people were beat by the police it wasn't always the policeman's fault because the people were not listening and were cursing at the cop." Thus, he concluded "everyone had made an excuse not to listen to each other. It was hard to argue against what I believed in—but I could see how both sides had good points—and how both sides only knew their side."

Nate noted another reason why some perspectives are resisted—seeing the world from some people's point of view can be "scary." Yet we argue that it may be critically important to assist students in their attempts to see the world from initially disturbing points of view—especially when they are trying to understand a topic like the Holocaust, which Nate and Carl were researching. Nate volunteered at one point to imagine he was a concentration-camp guard. It was a troubling realization for him that as a guard in a concentration camp he might have begun to enjoy hurting others. Nate recognized the potential corruption of power: "I could do whatever I wanted and [the inmate] couldn't do anything. Even in the drama I knew his arms were hurting and . . . there was a kind of enjoyment . . . like I was an animal or something waiting to pounce."

When students use drama as inquiry they imagine the world they are researching. They can experience how the world might look from the points of view of different key informants and dialogue from those positions. They can think and feel what it might have been like to have lived a different life in another historical or social context and, through shared imaginative encounters, students can understand more about times and places that seem initially remote. Students will often discover more than they had expected—this can also happen to us as teachers. When I imagined that I was a camp guard alongside Nate, I also caught a glimpse of evil and wondered how I would have fared if I had been born in Nazi Germany. If we use drama in our inquiries with students we need to expect such insights because, as Maxine Greene (1995) reminds us, "experience always holds more than can be predicted and . . . imagination creates openings to the unpredictable" (p. 45).

Community of Researchers

Professional researchers build a sense of community if they gather and interpret data together; they have common experiences to bind them together. As co-researchers, Jeff and I have discovered the strengths of sharing alternative views and forming common understandings, despite instances of initial confusion or disagreement.

Students must learn to cooperate and tolerate alternative views if they are to be co-researchers (11). Drama can be very helpful in creating community when teachers assist students in pursuing their research questions, and create opportunities for students to have significant shared experiences and periods of reflection. Rather than have abstract arguments, students can talk, disagree, and find common ground as they interpret shared drama experiences in the light of what they have read or been told by other people.

Collaboration Drama and inquiry only occur when students collaborate. In both, students must learn to share ideas, listen to each other, and build on each others' suggestions. Teachers support community-building when they help students listen to each other and focus on tasks, purposes, and deadlines. Jeff had helped his students learn to cooperate over the year; the process of making drama together in whole class sessions and in self-selected research groups (both with and without a teacher) helped to create a community of collaboration and caring about the work.

Many groups realized the cooperative nature and community building power of drama. As Mike said, "By doing the drama, we had to become a team and put everything we knew into our play book—for everybody." In subsequent research, each member of the group read different material and then shared information with the whole team. They cooperated in scripting scenes for their documentary but also critiqued each other's work. Mike explained the supportive tone of their critiques that were meant "to help the team. If one person knows more and plays better, the whole project is better for all of us."

Engagement Drama also helps students build a sense of community at a more basic level: shared engagement with the inquiry process itself.

If students agree to create drama together, they will begin with at least marginal engagement. Drama creates a space in which students are safe to ask questions and raise objections in role without feeling that their ideas are "wrong." Drama occurs in a fictional world where new ideas, attitudes, and perspectives can be explored without the social consequences of everyday life; students are not pressured to talk or move in public and should not feel judged or "put on the spot." As Heathcote stresses, though drama "demands . . . some change in understanding . . . it does this in a no-penalty zone of agreed depiction" (1984, 197).

If teachers build the sort of caring community discussed in Chapter 3, it will be difficult to "fail" at drama because passive participation is sufficient initially and students can be mentally engaged even when they say and do very little.

Further, drama encourages all students' participation because it is so inclusive, drawing on multiple modalities of learning and communication. Students who find reading and writing barriers to comprehension and communication are not excluded. Drama can include reading and writing but, as Jeff and I have shown, these activities always take place within shared contexts that students imagine and that thus support their joint examination of texts. As Pat, one of the boys working on the Mafia, reported, drama is not like "reading word for word. It's acting out what it means step by step . . . and trying things out to see what happens." Students, like Ned, who may be labeled "disabled," yet are skilled in talk or movement, can be community builders in drama; they can find that their abilities are valued by peers when they are the ones who can sustain or extend the possibilities of the world of inquiry.

In drama, students can come to know the world in multiple ways that go beyond the decontextualized interactions that so frequently dominate traditional classroom discussion. In drama, students can create the sorts of "multimodal" texts which Leland and Harste (1994) argue are essential in education. They can communicate with themselves and with each other using more of what Gallas (1994) calls the "languages of learning" than are used in abstract talk. There are many modes of communication and learning—many sign systems—that are usually marginalized or ignored in schools. Drama is a mode in its own right but also creates contexts that encourage participants to draw on other modes when, for example, they move, shape images, make sounds, tell stories, or use poetic language. The Mafia group, for example, at different times moved as if they were pushing handcarts, shaped a visual image of the results of the St. Valentine's Day massacre using my body, made the sounds of machine-gun fire, and began to retell the story of how they had paid protection money. At another time they might have moved to show the Mafia members' dreams and nightmares, or have written their tombstone epitaphs.

RESEARCH QUESTIONS

Researchers always have at least one question to motivate and guide their inquiries. Even though researchers change or modify their questions, if they did not have a motivating question that puzzles or worries them they would never begin to wonder, or talk, and then read, or write about a topic. As research continues, questions and focus become more specific. In schools where they learn to "follow directions" unthinkingly, students may actually have little internal motivation for their inquiries. By adopting different points of view, drama can help students look at a topic in new ways and uncover questions that interest them. Further, the process of using drama opens up perspectives and assists students to ask more complex or demanding questions which stretch them beyond their initial thoughts.

Finding Questions

Jeff's students were all working from broad research questions, which they had chosen in consultation with Jeff, and which had guided their extensive library research and information gathering. However, not all groups had a focused question to guide the creation of the video documentary which was to be the final synthesizing group project for the unit. Finding more specific questions was a major objective of the small group drama work which Jeff and I conducted.

I met with groups of students three weeks after they had begun their research. Initially, I talked with them in order to agree on specific questions that could be used to guide subsequent drama work. As they told me about what they had found out about their topics, some students were easily able to identify a more specific question that puzzled them, like the one noted at the beginning of this chapter within the broad topic of "Who was Al Capone?"

Other students who were unable to articulate more specific questions immediately did so after some initial work. In such cases, I used the materials they had collected to come to an agreement with them on a beginning point and waited for questions to arise. For example, the students interested in the Vietnam War suggested that they begin with a protest. I asked them where the protest would be held and they suggested a military recruitment center. I marched with the boys up and down the room and encouraged them to shout the slogans and sing lines from the songs we had just talked about. Then I switched to become a soldier trying to enter the center who belittled their efforts and questioned their position; they articulated many of the reasons for protesting the war, which they had previously formulated, along with hurtful comments about the recruiter. When I suggested that we all become military people inside the recruitment center, they agreed and from this point of view I asked them what we should do about the protests. The boys were quick to suggest that so long as they did not cause physical damage, they made little difference. As the boys later reflected on these and other interactions they realized that they were interested in the question, "What kind of protests were most effective?" This question then guided subsequent work and led to episodes that explored what happened when different people had to deal with protesters: a family with two sons (one a protester, the other in Vietnam); and a Pentagon policy committee over the years advising different Presidents on military buildup, bombing campaigns, the police, and giving advice about dealing with protesters at the Woodstock concert.

With other groups, a question became clear after the drama work began and I checked with the students that this was indeed what they were interested in exploring. For example, the group working on the Great Depression blamed me, in role as an out-of-work squatter, for not having a job. "There must have been jobs!" exclaimed one girl and the others tacitly agreed. The girls then acknowledged that they were all interested in exploring the question, "Why did some people not have jobs?" and later, "How were average people affected by the Depression?"

Changing Questions

All students who used drama wanted to change their research questions. In drama, they stepped into worlds of imagination, dialogued there, uncovered complexities, and realized the inadequacy of their previous positions and questions in light of the explorations they now needed to make. Anne (who had researched the Great Depression) noted on her end-of-year survey: "Drama helps you to answer unanswered questions. But it helps you ask new questions and add stuff that we didn't even know to ask about before."

The group researching the life of Hank Aaron realized in the middle of the drama work that rather than what Aaron had achieved in terms of sporting achievements they were much more interested in what he had to do to deal with racist attitudes. They recognized that the scripts they had developed for their video were basically reports listing facts (e.g., he and his brother would hit bottle caps with broom handles, toss burning rags back and forth, cut school to play baseball, and watch Negro League games) and three of the four boys found these scripts "boring." Over two sessions, the drama work concentrated on his experiences: in the locker room, receiving hate mail, with the owners, and with other baseball players in the Major League as well as in the Negro League.

During and after the drama the boys negotiated a series of new research questions. They had begun with the question: "Who is Hank Aaron?" but eventually settled on this question: "What did Hank Aaron have to do off of the ballfield to become great?"

Anthony said that "we realized that the most important things he had to put up with and get over were things like fighting through prejudice. If he couldn't do that then he could never be a great ballplayer. He did both and that's why he's great." Mike stressed that "The dramas made me realize that the research question about what he had to do was . . . well, we kind of thought we knew. I kind of thought it just had to do with practice, but now I see it had to do with being black and being great at baseball. It was overcoming prejudice and discrimination. [The library work and reading] was easy, the dramas and like . . . understanding [the inner experience of Hank] well, . . . that's what was really hard."

Ron and his partner, Buddy, asked themselves new questions both after their drama sessions but again as they used drama on their own in the preparation for their videotaping. They started their project with the preliminary research question: "What was the most important protest music against the Vietnam war?" After two drama sessions, the boys reviewed and changed their question to: "What kind of protests were most effective?" Ron explained to Jeff that, "we got to see that there were other ways of looking at it [the war] and so protests were not going to . . . like . . . automatically work." Buddy wrote in his journal, "So I will put both sides in my story, not just the anti-war side."

As they continued their independent research of the Vietnam War from "both sides," they added a question that acknowledged the way they had extended their attention: "How were people in the military affected by the anti-war protests?" As they prepared to videotape, they finally extended their attention to the broader question: "How can you change opinions to help peace?"

They scripted dramatic encounters, which extended their work with me; these involved a protest demonstration, musical and artistic statements, conversations, a family scene, a debate, and a letter-writing campaign. In their final video, key encounters dramatized arguments that both supported and protested the war in Vietnam; these included a family with one son in college and one in Vietnam, and a debate between two politicians.

METHODOLOGIES

Researchers have a host of research methodologies—or modes—available for the exploration of different questions. Different questions envision different outcomes or what John Dewey (1992) calls "ends-in-view" and thus suggest different major modes of gathering data.

Researchers interested in a question which necessitates facts and information are likely to employ quantitative methodologies. Their researcher stance will be more detached. Their research focuses much more on the "objective" details of situations rather than the "subjective" experiences of the people in those contexts. They will especially be interested in numbers and those details that can be "quantified."

As detached observers, the Hank Aaron group began their work with an interest in factual details and a quantitative stance. They interpreted their question "Who is Hank Aaron?" to mean: what records did he set as a baseball player? They read books for factual and statistical information, which they recorded in lists and notes. They were interested in the names of people with whom he had played, the number of home runs he had hit, and the different clubs for which he had played. The moves which Jeff initially made enabled the students to achieve their end-in-view: he helped them find books, locate information, and record details.

When researchers ask different questions, their mode of research often changes. If they are interested in people's experiences, they are more likely to conduct qualitative research during which they talk to informants (12). Because drama is always concerned with how people experience and interpret the world, drama can best assist in qualitative research.

Drama acknowledges and is respectful of students' experiences and their feelings of connection to others; it assumes that in concentrating on students' feelings as well as their thoughts, they will discover much that goes beyond what is described as "known" in the books they read. Alicia wrote about how drama assisted her as she became interested in meanings that went beyond the facts: "I learned how to ask more questions. I would ask questions like, 'How would I feel if I were in her place?' or 'How can I fit these clues together?' I would look back at things and try to figure things out."

Drama can also help with the motivation for quantitative research and assist students by creating contexts which help make sense of the factual details and numbers they discover. Mike noted that: "School is about facts—mostly boring facts; drama is about making facts exciting because you add the feelings . . . Drama takes facts and asks how they might have been different or how the facts might do something to you or someone else and how all that would feel. That's why I like drama."

In this chapter, I outline and discuss three broad modes of qualitative research: phenomenology, ethnography, and action research (13). These are listed below and contrasted with a quantitative research mode (14).

Categorizing students' questions using this table is useful for the teacher because different types of questions suggest different research methodologies and thus different ways of beginning and initially structuring drama

TABLE 5.1 Modes of Research

Mode	Question	End-in-view
Quantitative research	What are the objective facts?	Decontextualized information
Phenomenology	What are the lived experiences of particular people?	Contextualized personal individual meanings
Ethnography	What are the patterns of experience for people in general?	Contextualized shared social/cultural meanings
Action research	What action can I take to achieve a particular goal?	How action changes contexts and people

work. Jeff's students neither categorized their questions in this way nor overtly excluded any modes of research.

Although all modes of research are valuable, because each leads to different ways of gathering and interpreting data, using one mode exclusively privileges only one way of interpreting the world. All groups of Jeff's students had taken a mostly quantitative approach to the gathering of data. I initially wanted to help the students pursue one of the qualitative facets of their questions and began using either a phenomenological, an ethnographic, or an action-research approach (15).

These students' questions tended to be very general and could have led to the initial use of several research modes. As already discussed, I worked with them to uncover more specific questions that would suggest a way of structuring the drama work. With some groups, as the work continued, I switched modes when students wanted to follow a different direction or when I decided to raise different questions.

Phenomenology

The Hank Aaron group's research question concentrated on the life of an individual: "Who is Hank Aaron? How did Hank Aaron get to be so great at baseball?" Significantly, however, they had not considered how Hank Aaron had *experienced* his world. After a few minutes of talking about their topic it became apparent to me that the students were interested in the particular experiences of Hank Aaron—their research question could best be pursued using a phenomenological approach (16).

Phenomenologists describe and interpret the phenomena of personal lived experiences. "Phenomenology is the study of lived or existential meanings . . . it attempts to explicate the meanings as we live them in our everyday lives." (Van Manen 1990, 11). They may research their own or other people's experiences. Phenomenologists study themselves or other people in social settings, but they are ultimately intererested in people's unique, specific, personal experiences, and realities and are thus interested in personal stories and interpretations for their own sake. They ask a general interpretive question like "What are the lived experiences for particular people in particular contexts?" Their end-in-view is to understand and record the meanings that people make from their individual experiences in specific contexts.

A phenomenological approach to drama encourages students to focus on their experiences in drama worlds and to relate these imagined realities to how specific people might have felt. Drama experiences are imaginary, but they can nevertheless be deeply felt, personal, lived experiences—phenomenological experiences for the students. Part of the compelling nature of drama is the potential for students' "lived through experience." Reflection is important but without experience, students have nothing to reflect upon. As Dorothy Heathcote (1984, 97) notes, "Drama is about filling the spaces between people with meaningful [emotional] experiences . . . Out of these we can build reflective processes." Other boys in the Hank Aaron group later stressed the importance for them of trying to appreciate people's feelings and life experiences. One said that drama was "a good way to really get into it about what life was like and how it would feel." Another added, "you have to feel it before you can help someone else feel it."

All moves in the first Hank Aaron drama session were guided by the end-in-view of enabling the students to find meaning in the imagined experiences of one individual—Hank Aaron—and how he might have experienced contexts about which they had only read. I structured the work so that the students were able to experience the world of Hank Aaron from various perspectives but always reflected as researchers on the meanings of those experiences for him. Aaron became the primary informant in his interactions with others: playing baseball as a child, reading hate mail, in the major league locker room overhearing racist remarks, out in the ballpark hitting a home run, talking to the manager of the major league club, returning to his Negro League club, talking with his family, and reacting to white players. All four students represented Hank Aaron—two chose to do so for interactions with me or their peers. I took on roles with the four students as they created these contexts: a player, a relative, a manager, the voice of conscience, a narrator. Knowing that the students were asking a phenomenological question gave me an approach to our work; later I made reference to broader issues like institutionalized racism but initially I concentrated on Aaron's individual experiences.

After the drama work, the students reviewed their drama experiences and realizations. In preparing their presentations, the students scripted their own scenes, which drew on and extended the drama work. In addition to their role as Hank Aaron, they imagined they were people who wrote hate mail, sportswriters, Negro League teammates, white minor and major league teammates, baseball fans, and Aaron's family. They revised their research questions and continued their research as they reread material and altered their scripts. Interestingly, they began to ask themselves additional phenomenological questions: "How would Hank's experience have been different if he were white?" "What was his experience as a black ballplayer in a profession dominated by whites?" "How did the hate mail affect Hank and his family?"

Anthony explained how his group changed their priorities and realized the importance of considering Aaron's inner experiences in order to find out "what it was like for him." He noted that, "We realized that the most important things he had to put up with and get over were things like fighting through prejudice. If he couldn't do that then he could never be a great ballplayer. He did both and that's why he's great."

Other students asked phenomenological questions including:

What would be the effects of suffering through the Holocaust?
How were people in the military affected by the antiwar protests?
How were average people affected by the Depression?

Upon completion of his group's video, Mark said "It's kind of like history is really nothing but what happened to people." Phenomenologists agree. Abstract *talk* about experiences and problems cannot substitute for the complex situated *experiences* of people who are living through those problems. Rather than privileging any detached "objective" factual view as desirable, phenomenologists argue that the viewpoints of "subjective" experiences are essential if we want to record or find out how we, and others, actually experience the world. We interpret the world and adopt more detached perspectives as we reflect, but we cannot deny the importance of the intensity of experience or we will deny life itself and its importance as the object and tool of reflection.

Ethnography

If the students in the Hank Aaron drama had asked a question like "How did African-Americans in the 1950s cope with institutionalized racism in baseball?" then, I would have made quite different moves. If they had started from such a question, I would have structured the work so that the students would have examined the interplay of racist structures with fans, players, school children, and the game as a whole. I would not have concentrated on the experiences of one player. I would have made these moves because the students would have had an ethnographic, rather than a phenomenological, end-in-view.

Ethnographers are not only participants in everyday events, they are also observers of their social worlds. Ethnographers interpret social realities as they "participate, overtly or covertly, in people's lives for an extended period of time, watching what happens, listening to what is said, asking questions." (Hamersley and Atkinson 1983, 2). As participant-observers over a time, they participate in social events, but also observe what happens. They record what many informants do and say, interpret what seems to be going on from multiple perspectives, check their views against informants' interpretations, and thereby over time construct their own understandings about social and cultural realities (17).

Ethnographers can research in "foreign" cultural settings such as Bali or in familiar cultural contexts such as classrooms (18). They ask a general interpretive question such as, "What are the patterns of experience for these people in general?" Ethnography is complementary to phenomenology. The ethnographer looks for commonalities, whereas the phenomenologist looks for individual differences. Although the phenomenologist is interested in understanding a person's *particular* experiences, ethnographers end-in-view is understanding *general and shared* social and cultural realities. Ethnographers rely on the personal stories and interpretations of cultural insiders, but they are ultimately interested in these people's *shared* realities and social experiences. They are interested in understanding what holds people together culturally, their shared world views, and their general paradigms for action (19). They are also interested in the reverse—what views are not shared and what tears people apart. Ethnographers are always asking the general interpretive question "What is going on here among these people?"

Students are often just as confused about what is going on in the events described in books as any ethnographer might be in Bosnia. A thirteen-year-old trying to understand the behaviors of people in the world of major league baseball as the racial barrier was broken has tasks similar to those of an ethnographer trying to make sense of behaviors, relationships, and attitudes in an unfamiliar culture.

Students cannot *actually* do ethnographic research in societies from which they are separated by time and/or space, but it is useful to use ethnography as a metaphor to explore how students in drama can use drama to imaginatively research questions about other cultures or worlds that would otherwise be difficult or impossible for students to access. Like ethnographers, students in drama can explore and interpret imagined social contexts.

If the students want to explore an ethnographic question, then the teacher's moves will be guided by an end-in-view that concentrates on making sense across many interactions and from many social positions. A single perspective is insufficient—the students need to experience from *multiple* points of view as they play in an ethnographic key and try to make sense of a social context. In successive drama contexts, the students can depict the actions of various informants and like ethnographers they can interview them, observe them, overhear them, and other activities. When they reflect as researchers, they can try to generalize and look for commonalities of meaning and patterns of experience for the people in general.

For example, the Holocaust group had ethnographic questions. Within a broad interest in the culture of Nazism, they asked the question, "What was life like in the Nazi concentration camps?" The students clearly wanted to comprehend general patterns of experience in the camps—the end consequences of Nazi culture. They drew on and extended their understandings of the camps as they created the drama world. I was guided by an end-in-view of shared social meanings formed from multiple interactions that took into account different points of view. I wanted the students to experience the camps from multiple perspectives and find meaning in their reflections on this most horrific reality. They imagined the experiences of inmates as they were examined on arrival, as they sorted through clothing and shoes, as they tried to convince a guard to let them escape. I took on the roles of interrogator, organizer, and fellow guard. The students also looked at the camps and the inmates from other perspectives: the Germans who lived near the camps, survivors of the Holocaust, and Nazi guards. Those outside the camp were interviewed as potential witnesses at the Nuremberg trials—they were asked what they had seen and what they had known by me in role as an incredulous Allied officer. The guards contemplated the risks and pointlessness of trying to hide someone and the survivors remembered what sustained them.

Later, with minimal teacher participation, the students used drama as an integral part of their on-going research project into the culture of Nazism and its effects on those who were persecuted. They used the carousel strategy to observe and cross-examine each other from the perspectives of several real-life characters from Peter Weiss's *The Investigation*. They interviewed the dead about their past lives as Nazi kapos or as Eastern European Jews. Finally, they time-traveled into the camp at Auschwitz. Their project eventually led them to consider the culture of other historical and contemporary hate groups in America.

Like ethnographers, the students in reflection looked and listened for patterns across different people's experiences and views of their world. For example, though at first Carl in the Holocaust group had wondered why people did not escape from the camps, through the drama work he said he began to see a pattern of helplessness in the face of the scope of the Holocaust. He began to realize that the Holocaust "was so big. I knew it was bad, but not that bad. There were so many people. It was just so big and there was no escape." Though he had created drama with only three others, in his imagination he had begun to see, "How many were killed in one day because they were weak, old, tired of . . . for just *no* reason . . . just how many there were and how Nazis were so in control they could make up fake little things and contests and jobs so that they could make them suffer and kill them." He concluded that, "It was hard how it was like a game to kill and a game to stay alive." In attempting to make sense of the ongoing genocide and find a pattern, he used the metaphor of a game—one which was deadly and dehumanizing in very different ways for both perpetrators and victims. Carl was making social meaning about the Holocaust that was deeply felt with a breadth he had not previously demonstrated. However, his views were not treated as definitive—they were ideas that opened up discussion and led to additional research about resistance to the Nazis. In this sense, like ethnographers, the students were encouraged to return to their sources and review their tentative findings.

Other students were interested in the social and cultural realities of other groups of people from the beginning. Their questions suggested an ethnographic approach to the use of drama:

What was the Underground Railroad all about?
What was so bad about the Depression?
What were women's rights in the 1960s?

For other students, questions about the social and cultural aspects of their topics arose as a result of their research. Ron was particularly articulate about how drama helped him see the complex culture surrounding the Vietnam War. "[In the drama] I was inside so many different characters . . . the protesters, army, politicians, parents, Vietnamese people . . . We were so many people, we were everywhere. I didn't know there was so much involved, at first I couldn't understand how anyone would be for the war. It [the drama] kind of brought doubt. My original opinion kind of went down, then up again with some doubt. I had different reasons for my opinions, like the effect on the Vietnamese people which I'd never thought about—how they got killed and their houses destroyed and stuff . . . so in a way my opinion is stronger but it's less sure. I'm kind of more open to that there are other opinions that are strong and stuff even though you might disagree [with those other opinions]."

Action Research

The first session with the Hank Aaron group was structured phenomenologically to focus on Hank's individual experiences but by the second session the group's research question had taken an action-research turn. During the first session, the students had invented whispered racist remarks, hate mail, and veiled threats in the locker room. By the end of the session, Aaron (represented by Mike) had decided to quit and return to the Negro League, yet when I spoke as Aaron's conscience and asked if he wanted to be remembered as a quitter, Mike had paused, unable to walk out as he had planned. At the beginning of the second session, the boys wondered what else Aaron could have done in response to the racist attitudes he had experienced in the major leagues. They decided that he could not have just walked out because what he did would make a difference for other African Americans. The group's research question in effect had become: "What could Hank Aaron have done in response to racist remarks at that time and place in U.S. history?" Their end-in-view was now less concerned with the personal experiences of Hank Aaron and more with the choices he had made in response to racism. They were now thinking like action researchers.

Action researchers are, in a sense, hybrids between ethnographers and phenomenologists because they are interested, not only in the social realities of the culture of which they are a part, but also in their own experiences as they take action in particular contexts. However, in addition, they want to learn from their experiences in order to act more effectively in context to achieve whatever their aims may be.

When students reflect and wonder about what choices people had (or did not have) in particular contexts, they are entering an action-research mode (20). They have become interested in the differences people can make in a situation. A phenomenological approach concentrates on their experiences in situations, and an ethnographic approach stresses patterns that emerge across episodes experienced from multiple perspectives. An action-research mode focuses on both individual experiences and on sociocultural realities but additionally considers the interplay among individual or group actions, personal experiences, and social norms.

Action researchers' end-in-view is to consider how their actions change the context and effect the relationships among themselves and other people. As they reflect, they ask a general interpretive question such as, "What could I have done differently to achieve my goal?" Their actions are strategic. Their actions also change over time as they reflect and share their findings with others in their social situations. As Kemmis and McTaggart (1988) describe action research, it is "the way groups of people can organize the conditions under which they can learn from their own experience, and make this experience accessible to others."

Action research is recursive and reflexive with researchers examining and re-examining how situations affect actions and how changes in action change situations. Over time, they proceed in an "action-research cycle"— an ongoing spiral of steps: planning, taking action, observing, and reflecting. They make time for all four steps. They plan what their actions will be, act, observe how these actions seem to change the context and relationships between people, and reflect in order to make sense of what is happening and how they might alter their actions. The cycle then continues as further action is taken, which is itself reflected on.

If students have ends-in-view that resemble those of action researchers, then as teachers we can structure drama for cycles of action, observation, reflection, and planning. By manipulating time, the continuing spirals of action-observation-reflection-planning-action, can be speeded up or slowed down in drama. In the second Hank Aaron session, there were action-research cycles that spanned decades of his life in minutes. The students tried out several cycles of planning-action-observation-reflection-planning: explaining to his family that he could not quit, ignoring racist remarks, refusing to fight back, returning to talk to his former teammates in the Negro League. They repeatedly talked in and out of role to plan and reflect on action. They voiced his inner thoughts as he wondered about the effects of his actions on his family, Negro League players, major league players, and African Americans in general.

Action is inherent in drama. Indeed, the Greek word (dran) from which drama comes means action. However, participants will not be researching why people acted the way they did or how they might have acted differently, unless they reflect on the *meanings* of those actions (21). It is also important to note that "actions" need not involve overt movement but are reactions to an event which cause or permit other events to occur (Ball 1983, 11). Thus, silence, stillness, nonverbals, singing, and words are all actions; all can be reflected on (22). The boys showed Hank Aaron's feelings by how they imagined he hit a ball; at other times they were silent or inactive, as well as verbal, in response to racist remarks.

Mike's later comments highlighted how working as action researchers affected his understandings of Hank Aaron's choices and actions. "The dramas made me realize that the research question about what he had to *do* was . . . well, we kind of thought we knew. I kind of thought it just had to do with practice, but now I see it had to do with being black *and* being great at baseball. It was overcoming prejudice and discrimination. [The library work and reading] was easy, the dramas and like . . . understanding [the experience of Hank] well . . . that's what was really hard." Steven, conversely wondered about the actions of those who were prejudiced: "You just wonder why people act that way [prejudiced]; it's so mean."

Of course, few informants, whose perspectives students imagine, will have been professional action researchers. Some may have reflected very little on their choices and the consequences of their actions, but many have been acting like informal action researchers. The carefully orchestrated bus boycott in Birmingham, Alabama is a case in point. Rosa Parks may have been "tired" on the day she refused to move from a "whites only" seat at the front of the bus she boarded in 1955, but her act was not reactive and had been planned as a result of extensive reflections by the Women's Political Council in Montgomery (Kohl 1994).

When students evaluate their actions in drama they are not trying to recreate whatever happened in other contexts. They are imagining how they might have acted if they had been the people in those situations.

The teacher' role in using an action-research approach is to ensure that students have opportunities to focus on each aspect of the cycle; they need time both to take action as different people and to reflect on the consequences of those actions.

Ron and Buddy's initial research question ("What was the most important protest music against the Vietnam War?") had an action-research edge because the boys were interested in the role musicians and their music played in changing social attitudes. Over the course of their research, they changed their question several times but they retained their action-research approach—their final question became "How can you change opinions to help peace?"

Ron and Buddy continued to use drama after I worked with them as they explored "protest" actions in a variety of contexts: family disagreements, demonstrations, musical and artistic statements, conversations, debates, and a letter-writing campaign. In their final video, they dramatized arguments along a continuum between support for and protest against the war in their scenes of a family with one son in college and another in Vietnam, as well as in conversations and a debate between two politicians who disagreed about the war.

At the end of the project, both boys indicated an understanding of the complexity of the issue, and the sociocultural difficulties protesters faced in trying to change opinions. "It was hard to know what to do, but you had to do something, because you had to keep people thinking about it somehow," said Buddy. Ron told Jeff that, "It was important to me to see why people hated the hippies to see why some people didn't listen to them." Reflecting on his drama experiences, Buddy wrote that big protest demonstrations didn't work for his purposes because, "There was beatings and fighting when we wanted peace . . . and when the anti-war people were beat by the police it wasn't always the policeman's fault because the people were not listening and were cursing at the cop."

Some groups began with an ethnographic or phenomenological question but later wanted to explore action-research facets of their topic of inquiry. For example, the Holocaust group began wondering what life was like in the Nazi concentration camps but soon asked if prisoners in the camp could have escaped. The others imagined that they were sympathetic guards who discovered a person trying to escape and interacted for several minutes. They soon realized that they could neither easily hide him nor smuggle him out of the camp—there were thousands of other prisoners, hostile guards, and their own lives would be in danger. They reconsidered what action they might take and were at a loss to know what they could have done. Their initial assumption that escapes "ought" to have happened had been problematized.

Moving Among Different Research Modes

Finally, it is important to stress that *all* questions can be interpreted from quantitative, phenomenological, ethnographic, action research, and other research perspectives, and that each mode produces fruitful results. Students will initially be more interested in certain facets of their questions and, if we can discover these, we can use drama to assist them in their explorations. We begin with the approach that seems best-suited to the questions the students are asking.

However, we also need to consider when switching to an alternative approach seems appropriate. The students' interests may shift and as teachers we may want them to consider one of the other ways of making sense of the events they are researching. Students immersed in personal experiences will gain from considering cultural perspectives; students who are aware of how people are products of their cultures will gain from considering how individual actions can change situations (23).

OUTCOMES OF INQUIRY

Jeff's students had agreed to create videotape documentaries as synthesizing outcomes of their inquiries, which would be shown to all of their peers in the sixth grade. The documentaries had to both inform and inspire, provide information and questions about the topic and inspire some social action or transformed thinking about the issues. In their presentations, the students used drama as theatrical performances; the process uses of drama had been transformed into videotapes—products which were shared with their peers. When the students spoke with Jeff at the end of the unit about using "drama" in the classroom, they referred to both process and product without distinguishing between the two.

The students who used drama as inquiry created complex and engaging videos, which reshaped and extended the explorations with me or Jeff into scenes they scripted, revised several times, and taped. All students made multiple revisions to their presentations. One group completely refilmed their documentary four times. Troy noted that each time, "we added a lot more drama, because it lets the viewer get a way better grasp on your topic and keeps it interesting."

Clearly, the students had constructed complex understandings of the lives and worlds of the people they had researched, of the sociocultural contexts in which they lived, and of their possibilities for action in those contexts. Their understandings had been transformed and the students created products which were designed to inspire their peers.

Nicole was one of many students who recognized the generative power of collaboration in drama. Working on a video regarding women's rights, she explained that "you use the information you found out to make the drama. You have to know what the facts meant. If you didn't know, you could find out by making the drama . . . the point is that drama makes you know." Steven agreed, "We came up with almost all of our good ideas for the video by doing the dramas."

Using drama in the preparation of their presentation gave many students a keener awareness of audience. Sean noted that "drama is better at showing what life was like and helping people—other people like the audience—to experience it, too." Steven said that drama "could help people see better." Troy stressed that drama helped his group not only see "what would be interesting to put in the video" but also "what kind of things the audience would want to know and how to make it exciting for them."

Transformed Connections among People

A highly significant way in which students' understandings had been transformed was in their realization of human connections between their own lives and the lives of others. These connections seemed to inspire their thoughts about the possibility of social action and the need to communicate their new ideas with their peers (24).

Clearly, students connected with the lives of people who had lived at the times they were researching. In addition, many felt new connections between their research and their own lives in 1995 in a small Midwestern town in the United States.

Nicole wondered how the present would have been different if the historical figures they had researched had never lived. "It makes me think what my life would be like right now if there had been no Susan B. Anthony or Elizabeth Stanton."

Troy noted in his final portfolio letter regarding drama and his group's inquiry: "[Brian] not only helped us understand how Hank [Aaron] reacted, but also helped us understand how *we* may have reacted . . . So we understood Hank, but we understood because we looked at ourselves." Thus, the drama helped Troy to connect their research to his life, and also to perform the reverse operation, to connect his life to their research.

Drama helped many students apply their discoveries to their own lives, to make judgments and critical evaluations of the past, and to begin thinking about how individuals and groups might intervene and change situations.

The subsequent actions of Kristi's group illustrate what might happen when research makes issues come alive for students: They have the desire to do something significant with their knowledge, and will often act to do so. Kristi's group was so concerned about what they had learned about the treatment of women that they created a survey and posters that they used to create heightened awareness about the treatment of girls in the school setting.

The Hank Aaron group also began to realize that there were connections between the past and the present—similarities between America in the 1950s and in the 1990s. Significantly, their group had largely resisted the notion that racism still exists in America when they had begun the unit of study on Social Change and Civil Rights. After the drama work in which they imagined and talked about some of Hank Aaron's experiences with racism, these experiences became the focus of their video documentary. After completing their video, the group sought Jeff out to talk about how they might try to understand and address racism in the present. As Troy said, "What we're really wondering now is, what can we do about racism now?" Kristi made a similar point in summarizing the results of her group's research into women's rights: "Now we all kind of appreciate what the women before us did to get rights, and we all kind of want to know what we can do, too."

Other students recognized the ways in which we are also connected to people that stress our differences. For example, Kathy had originally assumed that anyone could find a job and had resisted the notion that people could not find work during the Depression. Eventually, she came to accept that living through the Depression was tremendously difficult, stressful, and very different from her own assumptions and experiences about finding employment. Christine admitted that "I didn't believe what I'd read . . . or what I'd been told." Her views had changed as a result of the drama work. "It was just totally different [from now]. It seems that maybe when things are tough, people get tougher . . . both tougher and kinder . . . people have to find the hard way to get by."

As Kathy reflected on her group's completed video she resolved to connect more with her grandparents. "Now I want to know how it [living through the Depression] changed the rest of their lives." She resolved to interview her grandparents during the summer to pursue that line of inquiry.

Tony also recognized connections with his family. During the creation of his video documentary with Robby, he said that "it [the drama work] gave me something to talk with my parents and uncles about. They had a lot of the same [conflicting] feelings about the war as I did. They talked a lot about being really frustrated. It made me think of how can you really change things."

Research Transformed

Robby was one of many students who had radically altered their views on research by the end of the unit. He said that during previous school experiences research was about "a topic—not really a question. We did a report kind of like a word find or scavenger hunt and the teacher is watching to see if we'll find it so you just go get answers as quick as you can. [With the drama, Brian] was watching to see what we'd find out . . . now we wanted to find out stuff so we kept redoing it."

Mike and Steven enthusiastically articulated their support of drama itself as a powerful research methodology. Mike said that "when we started doing drama, my attitude towards [the project] changed. All of a sudden it would be fun. We could do stuff. I thought about how to show it, what it meant and all . . ." Steven exulted that "Doing drama was Awesome Baby with a captial A!"

Like many students, Maria came to regard drama as integral to the inquiry process. "[Research] is about getting something to think about . . . I think that you should be trying to do drama anyway when you research— imagining what it would be like—but it's hard sometimes . . . Drama helped me because it gave me something to think about."

Tony was one of many who recognized the highly significant shift in the teacher–student relationship which occurred in Jeff's classroom over the year. Tony said that working together in drama was "working *with* a teacher instead of *for* a teacher . . . cuz he's helping you understand and do what we want to do." Tony had come to see his teachers as resources, and as co-researchers.

Inquiry Continues

Drama work helped students realize that inquiry is continuous. After working together to create fictional contexts, students often realized that they needed more information and additional perspectives. They then returned to the library or sought out other people with whom to talk. As students problematized their previous inquiry findings, they asked and then wanted to pursue further research questions. Further research was also prompted by questions that arose during or after drama sessions as students realized there were gaps in their knowledge.

The Great Depression group returned to their sources after imagining they were in poverty on the streets of a "Hooverville" slum in the 1930s. Their experiences in the drama were less concerned with not knowing what to do and more with realizing that their discoveries and reactions in the drama were in conflict with the expectations they had formed in their previous research.

Christine explained:

> When we started I didn't understand how all the people were so poor. I just thought they were lazy or something and that they should have tried harder to get a job, or should have moved where the jobs were. So then we tried it out in the drama and I couldn't get a job. Then I got one and somebody accepted less pay, and then only meals, but I had a family so I couldn't do that. And I moved, but I couldn't find work there either and in the end I lived in a cardboard box and I was really frustrated and angry . . . asking myself, "what could I do?" Then the health inspectors came and kicked us out . . . It really made me understand . . . I just didn't get it when I read about it.

Her group realized that they needed and wanted to know more about life in a Hooverville than they thought they did. They began the drama work with a very superficial attitude, saying that they knew about the slums and the difficulty of getting work. However, when they began to imagine living in a slum and tried to find and keep work, they became much more engaged with the topic and were eager to know more. I answered some of the group's questions, and shared what I knew about the difficulties of finding work in the 1930s. After working with me for two sessions, the girls returned to the library to do more research: they poured over WPA photos and at Jeff's suggestion read scenes from John Steinbeck's *The Grapes of Wrath*. In addition, two of the girls re-interviewed their grandparents. Previously they had conducted sketchy interviews whereas now they returned with a list of questions they wanted answered—questions that had arisen from the drama work. For example, they wanted to know what sorts of jobs people would be prepared to do in the Depression, how much work there really was, what choices people really had, and who might have ended up living in a Hooverville slum.

It is important to stress again that we are not suggesting that the students reached some final realization through the drama work. The students explored and raised questions in the drama, but these questions also focused further classroom investigations, which provoked further questions and more complexity. Students were re-searching. A few weeks later, after further research, Kathy's comments reveal some of the complexities of her thinking. "It was bad, but I don't think it was as bad as I felt it was in the drama—I'm sure there were things I could do but I couldn't see it then [in the drama]. At first I thought there had to be jobs somewhere, then I understood that it was worse than I thought at first, and I thought that it was really hard, but now I think that there had to be some laziness and there had to be some ways to find work . . . so I wonder what the government or people could do more of to help."

CONCLUSION

When I retell my experiences co-researching with the students from Jeff's classroom, people are amazed that students could have achieved so much in such a short time. I remind them of two essential aspects of the work. First, I was able to work so successfully with the students because over the year, an inquiry community had been established in the classroom. Drama can only work when groups want to "play" together in drama worlds and are not playing games like "get-the-teacher" or "impress-my-friends." These students had all come to see themselves as researchers, just as Libby had proclaimed herself a reader. They were serious about their topics and committed to their joint inquiries. Drama had become an important tool for them and they were eager to have me help them explore their ideas and questions using a method they had previously experienced as powerful, engaging, and thought-provoking. Second, they knew that their work would continue for weeks after I had left as they created their documentary videotapes and shared them with their peers. They had ends-in-view in addition to those which developed in the drama—they had assignments to complete and audiences they cared about with whom to share their results. Further, they had begun to care about how their work connected to the world beyond the classroom.

Organizing the curriculum around student inquiry has begun to be recognized as a powerful way to move students beneath the facts and beyond a skill-and-kill approach to learning. Inquiry that centers on students' questions and real world issues is intrinsically motivating, engages students in high level critical and creative thinking, and connects the classroom to the world—past, present, and future. Teachers are freed from being *the* authority to being *an* authority who can guide, assist, and wonder with students— but most of all we are freed to ask questions *with* students and join together in joint explorations.

Drama creates the conditions in which all of these facets of learning by inquiry can come together. However, drama does more because students and teachers together imagine alternative views, live through moments of these possibilities, and in dialogue each participant forges new understandings as they reflect on how the world—and they—might be different now that they have thought about drama realities in the light of the actual world. This happens if repeatedly we ask students, "From where you are now, how does this problem seem to you? And when it's been dealt with, let's look at where you now are" (Heathcote 1984, 121).

Drama harnesses imagination to open up new vistas: to see unexpected connections with people across time and space, change perspectives on those who seem close and those who feel distant, and always—to discover new visions of the future. As Maxine Greene stresses, when the imagination is released "no accounting, disciplinary or otherwise, can ever be complete. There is always more. There is always possibility" (Greene 1988, 128).

NOTES

1. Earlier versions of parts of this chapter appear elsewhere: Edmiston and Wilhelm (1996, 1998).

2. For a discussion of students and teachers as collaborative co-researchers and references to relevant research, see Clark and Moss 1996. For other examples of collaborative co-research with students of this age see, for example, Heath and McLaughlin (1993) and Oldfather (1993).

   For an illuminating discussion of drama as inquiry, see Gavin Bolton's afterword in Taylor (1996). Bolton acknowledges that drama can be used to conduct research provided students "already see themselves as researchers" in contrast to when the frame of researcher "is seen as something that can be hung around the students' necks as a temporary measure" (p. 193). He draws an important parallel between drama as research and Heathcote's mantle of the expert methodology (*see* Chapter 1). In both, the students' work is long term and they do not "pretend" to be researchers or experts, but actually regard themselves as such.

3. At the end of the project, the students viewed and evaluated their final projects, completed surveys, and discussed their drama work with Jeff. Most of the quotations from the students come from these data.

4. Professional researchers often "triangulate" their findings. Qualitative researchers frequently compare one person's interpretations (including their own) against another's; they repeatedly revisit their questions and assumptions in the light of these views. They may also gather data from multiple informants, multiple sources, and use multiple methods. Drama can similarly triangulate interpretations if students dialogue with each other and with themselves about their questions, findings, interpretations, and assumptions.

5. A broad distinction can be drawn between "qualitative" and "quantitative" research methodologies. Qualitative research is broadly synonymous with such terms as *naturalistic, interpretative,* and *constructivist* research methodologies. Ely and colleagues (1991) provide a useful overview of qualitative research methodologies. They note that rather than attempt to define what makes research qualitative, it is more useful to look at the methods that qualitative researchers use, which include holistic views of experiences of situations, immersion in settings, attempting to avoid predetermined views and seeking out informants' perspectives with a readiness to switch methodologies as needed. Qualitative research, then, has the aim of understanding experience as nearly as possible as its participants felt it or lived it" (p. 5). They quote Sherman and Webb's summary

   " . . . qualitative research implies a direct concern with experience as it is 'lived' or 'felt' or 'undergone'. . . ." When students are interested in "understanding [human] experience as nearly as possible as its participants feel or live it," then, they are engaged in qualitative research (Sherman and Webb 1988, 7).

   In contrast, however, quantitative research frequently operates within a "positivist" paradigm. Positivistic research was originally grounded in the natural sciences in which the aim was to be "positive" and "objective" about results. Observations are reduced to numerical order and other "objective" data—the facts; "subjective" perspectives and interpretations of researchers or "subjects" are assumed to be at best unimportant, or at worst, biases that must be discounted. By contrast, qualitative researchers argue that when we ask questions about how human beings interact or understand—the quality of their experiences—it is essential to discover the perspectives and experiences of actual people. Thus, they insist that researchers must discover the subjective experiences of informants.

   Jeff's students were interested in "facts" but were much more concerned with the "quality" of the lives of the people they were researching. In talking about research, unless otherwise stated, from now on in this chapter I will be talking about qualitative research.

6. I should stress that many researchers attempt to maintain an "objective" stance in "studying" their "subjects"—they try to minimize any effects on their inquiries.

7. Drama enables this because of its liminal nature; it exists on the boundary between the individual imagination and the external world. Again, I should stress that the use of drama is not a technique which professional researchers use.

8. I am using the term text to mean written information, including books, newspapers, documents. Clearly, some texts are more accessible to proficient readers.

9. As discussed in Chapter 1, participants experience a kind of "double consciousness" in drama—an experience, at the same time, of being in both the actual world of the classroom and the fictional world of the drama—which makes it possible for students to reflect in internal dialogue on their experiences.

   When drama is used for inquiry students' double consciousness can also be experienced as a double stance of researchers and informants. If, like Jeff's students, the participants are committed to conducting inquiry then they will regard themselves as researchers. If they become engaged in a drama world which is built on the world they are researching then the students will experience from the perspective of people who are "informants" for their research. Both of these realities are experienced at the same time since the students never forget that they are researchers in the classroom; if they are engaged in the drama work they also continually see the world from other perspectives. At any moment the teacher can highlight the students' attention on one or other of these stances.

10. The students were aware that we were also conducting research in the classroom and were eager to help in giving their responses to drama work. However, we did not formally share our research questions with them.

11. Wells and Chang-Wells (1992) describe at length classrooms where students are learning collaboratively by inquiry. At the core of each of those classrooms is a "community of collaborative inquirers" with "the values of caring, collaboration and curiosity."

12. I am not suggesting a clear split between qualitative and quantitive research since the same professional researchers often use both methodologies. I am noting that the *questions* which researchers ask are best answered by different methodologies.

13. Other qualitative research methodologies include: biography, history, life history, philosophy, curriculum criticism, and critical theory. The three chosen seem to most closely parallel drama work.

14. We do not intend these descriptions to be more than a cursory introduction to these methods of conducting research. The description of each mode deliberately avoids the complexities of these approaches since we only intend to propose a template rather than a detailed analysis of different research modes. Nor do we wish to suggest that these research modes are hermetically sealed off from each other since, in practice, researchers in one primary mode will often draw on many other methodologies.

15. I should stress my own role as an action researcher and reflective practitioner. When I was teaching I had my attention on the students' needs as a teacher and wanted to help them in pursuit of their questions. Though I had begun to sketch out the idea of a framework of different research modes, my realizations about the usefulness of this categorization occured later. In teaching I intuitively drew on my experience as a teacher (and as a researcher) as I helped shape the students work. My detailed awareness of the precise framework explored in this chapter came later.

16. Again, I should make clear that I did not share this terminology with the students. I focused their attention on their questions.

17. We use the term "culture" in a very broad sense to mean any social context which has shared social meanings not apparent to the researcher. The purpose of interviewing others, watching them, and engaging with them is to discover aspects of these shared meanings—why people do what they do.

18. It is worth noting that ethnographers who work in apparently "familiar" settings like classrooms must make the familiar "strange" so that they can begin to see

patterns where these may have previously been invisible. Heathcote (1978) compares how Brechtian theatre and her uses of drama in the classroom both work in similar ways to make the familiar strange.

19. An ethnographic "thick description" (Geertz 1973) foregrounds the researcher's outsider perspective as she interprets, analyzes and identifies structures of meaning which may not be apparent to insiders.

20. The potential for students as action researchers has been recognized (Coe 1993) by a teacher who advises her students to "think for yourself" and who wants them to become "more thoughtful and reflective in their work." Stevenson (1986) has also noted how teachers can collaborate with students in the teachers' action research projects.

21. Note reflection and action can occur at the same time. For a detailed description see my 1991 thesis and the work of Schon, especially Schon 1983.

22. For a discussion of dramatic action see, for example, Ball (1983) who defines dramatic action as "When one event [which could be words] causes or permits another event, the two events comprise an action"(11).

23. In addition, students' research will be intensified if the work is structured as a spiral so that the students are re-searching for answers and re-considering the implications of their questions. As described, this was something that happened for groups studying the Vietnam War, the Concentration camps, and the Depression.

24. Their peers, in fact, gave them the highest possible rating for "audience consideration" as well as for "interesting and informative content"—two of the five criteria agreed upon by the class and Jeff.

6

Drama Across the Curriculum

Jeffrey D. Wilhelm

I used to think that good historians and good scientists and people like that were all like good students—good at following directions and doing things according to a formula or a plan or something, following rules, you know . . . now I think that good students and scientists and people like that have to think new things and make things, they have to, you know, like we did, design things . . . figure things out and make things.

—Mark, 7th grade, at year's end

BRAVO, DRAMA!

All of our arguments for using drama are about the necessity of student ownership, situated learning, and model building in education.

Drama helps students to own their learning; drama comes to personally involve them in that learning; it helps them to experience and express their learning as a story. White (1981) tells us that defining and using narrative takes us to the very core of culture and humanity. He cites Roland Barthes, who writes: "Narrative is simply there, like life itself, international, transhistorical, transcultural . . . [It] is a human universal on the basis of which transcultural messages about the nature of a shared reality can be transmitted. Here . . . the events seem to tell themselves" (p. 3). Telling stories, like those we tell through drama, is our most direct and basic way of organizing, exploring and expressing our human experience. Hardy writes (1977, p. 21) that "narrative is a primary act of mind."

Drama, because it weaves an experiential story about questions of great significance, serves to situate learning and give it a context. In drama, students know what they are learning, why they are learning it, and what it might come to mean for them.

Drama also requires the creation of a "drama world," of a rich mental model that expresses a theory of the world, that seeks to express a map of how things work or could work, and that is generative in that it informs our understanding of new phenomena. Models are a form of analogy; aspects of the model refer to and map onto aspects of the represented phenomenon. A model strips away all that is not theoretically interesting in order to understand that which is most significant. Drama provides a microscope for studying that which is most relevant.

This clearly ties in to new visions of the curriculum as a journey to mastery of the generative processes of learning.

It is clear that drama works well to serve all of these purposes when applied to human and cultural concerns in the domain of the humanities. But how could it help to teach important conceptual understandings in math and the sciences? In these areas, concepts are fairly content specific and are not open in the same way to human interpretation. In this chapter, we explore how drama can serve conceptual understanding in content domains precisely because it involves students personally in their learning, situates cognition, and helps them to make the abstract accessible as they create and revise mental models that serve as tools in the service of constructing and testing understanding. Drama provides a potent avenue for model building, because drama itself is a representational device. Drama provides students with a process for designing, applying, debating, evaluating and revising what they know, which contrasts with the simple reception of knowledge that is expected when information is simply transmitted to them. We already know which process results in measurable learning.

DRAMA AND SCIENCE

I have had the great fortune the past two years to work closely with my friend Rand Harrington, a science educator at the University of Maine, in a variety of settings in which we have been able to use drama. In a very satisfying way, my work with Rand and his own or our shared students represents the completion of a circle. Brian assisted my own teaching performance using drama until I began to use it on my own. Even then, I would return to him for advice and further help. Now that I have achieved a measure of intersubjectivity with Brian and other established drama practitioners, I am quite competent at using drama on my own. Part of that expertise is lending my consciousness and support to others, such as Rand and classroom teachers like Jane Theoharides in Lincoln, Chris Prickitt in Dexter or Jan Banks in Belfast, Maine, all of whom have begun using drama in their own classrooms.

Rand's schtick is learning "Physics by Inquiry" and he is certainly one of the nation's foremost practitioners of this approach. In order to teach through inquiry, Rand insists on the necessity of profound teacher content knowledge. He told me that "You must be more expert than the students to lead inquiry, because you have to model, question, and structure their work to lead them down the path of continual progress toward more sophisticated and accurate understanding."

One of Rand's purposes in teaching physics by inquiry is to help students develop into what he calls "intelligent novices." Such a student can go into a new situation and create meaning. The most important skill for intelligent novices to possess is the metacognitive ability to recognize when they truly know something. They need internal mechanisms for testing knowledge. "They have to be able to generate and test out models for physical systems," is how Rand put it. "Drama is a tool that helps them create models. It's also a feedback tool for testing understanding. It helps them recognize when they've achieved functional understanding." Drama, Rand argues, provides a "direct experience that is necessary to deep understanding. This experience helps to develop a pure physical insight that comes from an ability to visualize, test and understand what is going on."

Rand uses an entirely hands-on process orientation in his teaching. He matches instruction to students' current understandings with an eye to what they need to know. A prerequisite for this kind of teaching is coming to understand the nature of student misconceptions. Strong preconceptions, or mental models, of how electricity works make it very difficult for students to learn about electricity from reading or hearing about it. Their erroneous models are flexible and seem to accommodate incongruous ideas. And, Rand says, you can't create experiences that address how kids are thinking until you know how they are thinking. This is one way in which he uses drama.

Rand uses the same underlying frame for instruction that I have long used in my humanities classrooms. First he elicits students' prior experiences and beliefs (E = experience), confronts them with the appropriately challenging physical phenomena (T = testing with new or discrepant data), and then helps them to resolve the schism into a new and more accurate model (R = response). As he goes through this process, he has found drama a way to "engage the kids at a deep level, so they will want to resolve the discrepancy between their beliefs and their observations."

Thus, his first task as a teacher is to get students to make visible their deep-seated mental models. He uses drama for this, and then uses drama to challenge them, offer alternatives, and finally to guide them toward a resolution that instantiates learning.

The Electric Company

This past summer, Rand directed an Electricity Institute for Teachers at the University of Maine. After some initial hands-on instruction, he asked small groups of teachers to create an *analogy drama* that would provide an analogy for illuminating how electric current behaves in a simple electrical circuit.

After the drama, the "characters" were to attend a kind of *press conference,* in which they would explain the meaning of their drama and would engage in a critical dialogue with the rest of the class about the usefulness of their analogy.

One group created a drama in which they were adolescent eels. These eels represented electric charges that had been stimulated to dance and move about by a "party"! The adolescent eels' energy was fueled by trips to the fridge, which represented the battery. Without food, or energy, to stimulate the party, "the fiesta ain't happening! It's over!" There were two resistors to the party, the two parent eels, both of whom represented light bulbs. There was a door to the party, and in typical adolescent fashion, the more the resistance, the more eels—or charges—came through the door. This in turn made the parental units angry, and the more charges that ran through their circuit and to their battery, the brighter they got.

The class was thoroughly amused by this drama "model" of an electric circuit. Rand loved it too, and it served his purpose of revealing his students' misconceptions. Some elements of the model were consistent with what students had observed about electrical circuits during the first two days of class. Other physical phenomena were belied by their model. You see, the number of charges in a circuit remains constant; this number does not change. And lightbulbs do not get brighter because there are more charges, but because the charges are moving faster.

At this point, Rand began brainstorming for ways to construct experiences, observations, experiments, and dramas that would get these students to reflect on what they had done so they could recognize the inconsistencies in their model and come to realign them.

His dramatic interventions included providing alternative models or *physical reenactments* of the electric circuit. "Let's reenact some other models and see how they work," Rand suggested. In the first, Rand became the battery and he asked students to sit in a circle that included him. They played the part of the conducting wire. Rand passed ball bearings that simulated charges around the circle. They did this for a while, when Rand asked two students to become light bulbs and asked them how they, as resistors, would behave differently than the others who were playing the part of the wire. Based on their responses, Rand suggested that they each stick a ball in their pocket for every few balls that came around. Not long after this began, students began to critique this model. Fewer balls were getting to the second light bulb, yet they had observed that a second lightbulb on any given circuit would have the same brightness as the first. How could that be if the charges they received were different?

Then another problem occurred. Fewer balls were getting back to the battery. So lightbulbs should quickly dim. Again, this did not match their observations.

The students posited that the battery could provide an endless supply of charges and that the light bulbs would use very few of these, though this would eventually deplete the battery. So Rand set up another reenactment involving the tearing off of sheets of toilet paper. More critique followed.

Eventually, Rand set up a final model. There was a circle of rope, which the students, as conducting wire, held lightly in their hands. One student played the role of the battery. Was he the source of the rope? No. His job was simply to move the rope. His role did not involve creating charges. The rope was made taut so if it moved at one place in the circuit, it would move everywhere because all charges move at once. Interaction was consistent along all points in the circuit.

The circuit was broken. Everything stopped.

Light bulbs were added, and these students, as resistors, felt they should hold the rope more tightly. Their hands got so hot, they dropped the rope. "If you held on any longer, your hands would be glowing!" Rand joked.

The students decided that energy was dissipated at the point of the resistor, but differentiated this energy from the charges. They came to the conclusion that this model worked better than the others. They further concluded that the battery is a source of energy that causes the flow and pushes the charges. "The battery provides energy—not charge!" After comparing this latest model with their observations in the lab, the groups were asked if they could revise their original dramas.

The eel group got quickly to work. The party became closed. The eels who were there had to stay until bedtime and no other eels were allowed in. The door was locked so there would be no path for extra charges. There was a line to the refrigerator and the fridge door pushed the eels through the circuit as they entered and left. Everyone had a good laugh and agreed that a more accurate model had been created.

Rand described a teaching strategy that matched the E-T-R model. "First, I provide them with experiences in the form of experiments and observations of the phenomenon. In this case, I gave them batteries and wire and bulbs and asked them how many ways they could light the bulb. Then we created more sophisticated circuits and such. Eventually, I wanted to assess their internal model, so I had them create the analogy dramas (E). It's amazing how often students are not learning what you think they are learning. So I provided other incorrect but probable models to help them, by comparison, to see the relative strengths and weaknesses of their own model. (T) Then, based on their critiques and discussions and new observations, I guide them to create a new model (R). I offer as much prompting as they need. In the end, they have to justify every element of their model relative to their observations. I don't let them talk about electrons and things they've never seen. The model has to look like, well, like what a circuit looks like when you observe it. And you have to understand what work the model does and what work it doesn't. You have to be aware of where and how far the model maps onto the actual phenomenon. The students here learned the concepts involved in electrical circuitry, but they also learned how to create models."

One of the teachers in the institute was a high school teacher who had taken physics courses as an undergraduate. At the conclusion of the drama sessions, he told Rand that he had "learned more in two hours here than I did in all my college physics courses."

Sixth-Grade Studies Motion

Earlier in the year, Rand, Rand's graduate student Steve Kaback, and I joined Chris Chilleli at Orono Middle School to teach a three-week kinematics unit on uniform motion.

Early in the unit, the students were busy setting up experiments and recording their observations. The task asked for students to create uniform motion (motion that neither speeds up nor slows down), using a ball on a steel track. In the beginning, the students used only their physical senses to judge whether or not the ball stayed at the same speed. Some thought the motion was uniform when the "track was flat." Others thought the motion was uniform when the sound of the ball on the track stayed the same. After a lot of discussion and experiments, many students concluded that uniform motion was impossible. Later the students had access to meter sticks and stop watches, but only some used it to test their hypotheses.

After several different kinds of trials with the ball and track, the students had composed an operational definition of "uniform motion." I wanted to elicit the students' beliefs about uniform motion and get them to commit, however tentatively, to a model. To this end, I used the *continuum* and *radio show dramas*. I asked the question: "Is uniform motion possible?" I asked students to line up on a continuum from those who believed most strongly that it was not possible to those who believed most strongly that it did exist. In order to place themselves within the continuum, the students had to converse with each other about their beliefs. When the line was formed about five minutes later, there was a very even distribution between those who were sure uniform motion was possible, those who were sure it was impossible, and those who weren't sure. The line was strung out except for a clump of four students at the "know it's possible" end who were all positive that uniform motion happens. They therefore occupied the same position on the continuum.

I then did a radio show as a talk show host. "Today we have a hot topic on our call-in show, Motion Happens! The issue is, does uniform motion exist? Caller number one, what do you think?" As students committed to a belief, I asked them why they held it. Interestingly, the students at the "know it's possible" end all used evidence they had garnered with stopwatch and measuring tape. "This is what I measured," was what they had to say. On the other end, the students articulated what boiled down to philosophical perspectives. "Things are always slowing down because of inertia." "It's gotta be speeding up or slowing down. Things are always doing one or the other—you're either living or dying." "If you put the track up, the ball speeds up. If you put it down, it slows down." The continuum was then folded, so that those who disagreed most strongly in the possibility of uniform motion were talking to those who agreed most strongly. Students were asked to be physicists at a conference who were debating this issue.

After a few minutes, we asked what arguments they had heard. Which arguments would carry most weight with scientists and why?

I noted that many students were changing their opinion on uniform motion. Many who had not used the stopwatch returned to their track to experiment. Others rewrote their operational definition of uniform motion.

In a short drama episode, I elicited their beliefs, confronted those beliefs with those of others, and many students then continued on to do the kind of work that resulted in a revised belief and mental model regarding the topic at hand.

Drama activities were used throughout the unit. At the unit's conclusion, the students took on the role of police tracking the speed of cars traveling along the road in front of the school. The local police came to help out, and used their radar and triangulation equipment to compare their findings with those of the students, who had only stopwatches and their mental models to guide them. One group of sixth graders clocked the moving police car at a speed that was only one-hundredth of a m.p.h. different than that clocked by the radar. All groups were within one mile per hour of the police's readings. A workable and shared model had been achieved!

In an interesting twist, the kids turned out to have a much more thorough and accurate understanding of motion than the television reporter who came to film a segment of our work for the evening news. Though the students described "rate" to him as "distance over time", he—perhaps the victim of an erroneous mental model—proceeded to describe rate as "time over distance"—a mistake that made the students and ourselves most gleeful.

The final project for the unit was to create a video documentary about a "uniform motion" question of the students' own. Students took on the roles of investigative reporters to reveal the speed that cars traveled in residential areas, and of ESPN sports announcers determining how fast a hockey puck can travel, and if it indeed ever travels at uniform motion on its way to the net. One group of students revealed that they were failing to maintain their accurate model of uniform motion by asking how many free throws could be made in one minute. As teachers, we used questioning and comparisons to classroom events to challenge their error and to provide them with the "legs" to bring their model back in line.

When Chris Chilleli presented our work to the New England region conference of the National Science Teachers Association, he was picked as one of two presenters to go to the national conference to report on how instructional innovations could be used to meet the national standards in science. At the national conference, one NSTA official remarked to Chris that this was the first unit he was familiar with that actually guided students to understanding in a way consistent with the national standards.

As teachers, we had asked the students to do science, to create theoretical models, to confront inconsistencies, and to revise interpretations. When students experienced difficulty, we had provided data, materials, challenges, support, and other kinds of instructional assistance to serve as "legs" to extend their reach.

The drama helped students to develop extra "legs" by making the models real and concrete. As Tharp and Gallimore (1988) report "[abstract] schooled concepts, systems and general principles can only be connected to the world through the [concrete] everyday concepts that have risen through practical activity" (p. 107). To master abstract "schooled concepts" requires active reflection and conscious attendance—this was achieved in these cases through drama work. Tharp and Gallimore go on to argue that this relating of the everyday to the schooled allows everyday concepts to become autonomous tools for thought. When this happens, Rand's goal for his students is achieved.

A POTPOURRI OF DRAMA

I have had many other experiences with drama across the curriculum that engaged students and helped me to assess their understanding, provide context for their learning, and allowed me to know how to intervene appropriately as I guided them on a path of continual progress toward mastery.

As a teacher of German, I had both fifth graders and high school students role play problem situations through their use of the German language. As one example, students would create situations that they foresaw for themselves: that they had to take a business trip to Frankfurt and take a taxi to the Ratskeller where they would have a business lunch with the president of a German bank. They would be expected to order and pay for the meal, and to strike a deal. Students scripted and role played these kinds of dramas. Often, I would enter the drama world as the taxi driver or German bank president to see how flexibly they could deal with the problems I would introduce.

My friend, Bill Anthony—now a professor at Northwestern University—inadvertently introduced me to process drama for language teaching. Under his guidance, I created a drama each Wednesday during which the classroom was turned into a German restaurant, soccer stadium, or marketplace where only German was spoken. On other occasions, we became Germans hiding Jews or experienced the Nazi Putsch in Munich. We performed scenes from Brecht's *Mother Courage*, and wrote reviews in role as political analysts.

As a geometry review, I hosted a *Job Fair* for geometric concepts. Students took on the roles of concepts or functions and composed cover letters, resumes, and references for themselves. They then went to a job fair and attempted to get employers to hire them by explaining and proving their usefulness. One exchange I remember was the concept of "Area" trying to get a job with a roofing contractor by explaining that he could "calculate how many squares of shingles you'll need." Employers had a certain amount of money and tried to hire as many useful concepts as they could with their funds. The concepts held out for the highest bidder as they justified their usefulness.

In the Life Sciences, a group of us had the students draw a classroom-sized human body in the activity room. We then drew in organs and systems. In an *Incredible Voyage drama,* we became the brain, hemoglobin, bone marrow, or moving blood cells. Students acted out where they were and what they were doing there. We would then stage problems like infections, arteriosclerosis, or a compound fracture of the leg. Students would have to rush to the scene and act out how the body would react.

Rand described to me a similar *Magic School Bus drama* in which the school bus would get morphed into a biscuit eaten by a dog, or a water molecule entering the water cycle. Students would take on the roles of the biscuit, intestine, stomach acid, among other things to act out and comment on the physical changes taking place.

Integrating language arts with the sciences or math, I have sometimes asked students to become an authority who writes a children's book about a phenomenon. The authors then present their stories in role to their elementary school reading buddies. On one occasion, the authors staged *a book signing* and stayed in role as they read their story, answered questions, and interacted with their learning buddies.

I once helped students to write a historical melodrama based on their Depression research, complete with period music. On other occasions, we staged a *Tunnel of Time,* in which the audience would enter a time warp in which they interacted with different historical figures who reenacted brief events or held conversations with them. My colleague Nancy Cook has students create a medieval *wax museum* in which each student takes on a medieval role. When visitors during Open House step on the button on the floor, the wax figure acts out her daily role and provides information about her life.

I have also had success engaging students in game-like dramas like *Meeting of the Minds* and *Quiz Show* in which they would take on expert roles and interact with others. When studying the Industrial Revolution, the Greek myth of the Golden Age, or the Oregon Trail, I would ask students to engage in dramas I called *Dreams of the Future, Dreams of the Past* (cf. O'Neill and Lambert 1982) in which they would reflect, from a particular point of time, on their past and future, role-playing past events and envisioning future possibilities. This usually led to the writing of poetry.

Simulations also work well. I have purchased and used simulations through companies such as Interact and have written some simulations of my own. One of the most memorable was during a year I taught in boarding school when we did a simulation of Puritan life. Three boys were made Elders who could enforce the Puritan mores regarding dress and behavior. They outlawed drinking soda, deeming it impure—for everyone but themselves and made mandates about appropriate feminine attire, but none for boys. There was a sophisticated reporting system for informing the community about offenders. Because everyone lived on a closed campus, the students were held accountable for "moral" behavior at all times during the week we simulated.

During our daily "town meetings," the Elders ostracized offenders and made them wear "scarlet letters" or "bad bags." The girls in the class became very fed up with this after a few days, but the Elders were the supreme authorities. Many complaints were made about them, but they threw these away. In class, we ran a Puritan school in which we used the Common Book of Prayer as was used in the seventeenth century. Failure to learn one's lessons brought shame and punishment on the family. The boy in role of the preacher delivered a sermon that excerpted Jonathan Edwards' "Sinners in the Hands of an Angry God." It was an engaging experience and helped these tenth graders to grasp their later reading of *The Crucible* with a new intensity. I noted that they were continually making connections between the simulation and the reading that followed. I could go on, but why? I'm sure you have the idea.

DRAMA AND LITERACY

Drama provides some badly needed opportunities for students to exercise and develop new ways of knowing. Gardner's work (1982, 1983) has helped to debunk the notion that there is one way of learning, or that there is such a thing as a fixed IQ. Gardner suggests that instead of asking "How smart are you?", we should ask "How are you smart?" School should be a place where students are encouraged to use their natural talents and aptitudes and to develop aptitudes they may not yet possess. This means that as teachers we must widen our own repertoire in order to create new opportunities to guide student performance, and new avenues for students to explore and express their learnings.

Drama also helps to develop a critical literacy because it helps students to look inward to define the self; to imagine and enter the selfhood and perspectives of others; and finally, to look outward to critically read and converse with the world, open always to change and transformation and to working toward these transformations. Such a dialogue, in Bakhtin's sense, allows the reader/actor a sense of agency, and the ability to "rewrite" and help transform her own understanding, herself, and her world. Being literate, that pursuit of reading and conversing with the world's many 'texts' continually develops these three abilities I would call "self-definition," "social imagination," and "critical literacy."

Literacy is the willingness and the ability to evoke, conceive of, express, receive, reflect on, share, evaluate, revise, and negotiate meanings in the various forms that these meanings may take. Drama is both a way of making meaning, and an extension and support to the meanings we make when we read, talk, and explore the world. Drama is a way of learning through body, mind and soul.

IT CAN WORK FOR YOU

A lot of people who know me are surprised that I make use of drama in my classroom. I'm not particularly flamboyant, and if I have any claim on an artistry, it's certainly of a more introspective kind. I was never trained as an actor or as a drama educator, and I never had any extensive experience in theater. Though making use of short role plays and improvisations seemed quite natural to me, I was often uncomfortable when I first began to use extended process dramas with my students. But with Brian's support, I pushed on through, and I learned how to frame dramatic scenes. I learned how to build on what students had done in one episode so that it could be made to follow some kind of inner logic *and* be made to serve my higher purposes for the lesson and for learning in my classroom. Now, I regard drama as one of the most powerful teaching tools at my disposal and I constantly use it with both forethought and in the spontaneous moments of possibility that so often come up when working with kids.

A lot of my friends and colleagues seem to resist the idea of using drama as somehow foreign and unnatural, yet dramatic play is as natural a way of learning as there is. This is obvious not only from a look at the work of the giants of developmental psychology, but from everyday observation in our living rooms, front lawns or classrooms. Why shouldn't drama and play remain a natural way of learning, and of teaching? We only have to overcome our traditional and very tired notions of what a school is, and what should happen in a school to bring dramatic learning to life.

Whenever people complain to me that they'd like to try classroom drama, but that it doesn't really fit their style or personality, I'm reminded of an experience I had as a young teacher. I was in my first job, working as a high school English teacher in Baltimore, Maryland. Typical for a young teacher, I was coaching cross-country and basketball, advising the literary magazine, and fulfilling a whole host of other duties. One day, while running with some kids on the road that circles the campus of Johns Hopkins, I slipped on a piece of ice, and I could feel a little bit of give behind my knee that gave me the sensation of something slightly popping or ripping. But on I ran, though the pain became a little worse and began to throb.

At home, I iced my lower hamstring and gave exercising a rest for a few days, when I set out again. This time, I experienced excruciating pain and had to walk home. A week later, I could actually run, but the leg still hurt, and I certainly couldn't fully extend it or do any sprinting. After about four weeks of this, I was really frustrated and suffering a bit of physical agony to boot. That's the first point of the story, I think, that I kept running on legs that didn't work, because they'd worked for me in the past, hadn't they? I resisted the notion that a new intervention might help me. But I finally capitulated and asked around at school for a doctor.

I had a stroke of good luck. It turned out that the school's team doctor was Dr. Les Mathews, an orthopedic surgeon at Memorial Hospital, who worked very closely with both the Baltimore Colts football team and the Orioles baseball organization.

I went in one Saturday morning to the sports medicine complex and was led by a trainer through a series of weight machines, exercise bikes, and resistance machines. The trainer carefully charted the results of every test, checking first my right leg, then my left, then both legs together. He handed me a folder with all the results and directed me to Dr. Mathews waiting room.

It didn't take the good doctor long to diagnose my problem once he had a look at the results of my tests. He knew the exact muscle (right down on the bone, he said, running from the knee on down into your hamstring) that was ailing, and exactly how it was ripped. He began to outline a training regimen of intensive weight lifting and stretching. He filled up two sheets of paper with exercises to be done and handed them to me. "There you go," he said, "do all of these each day and in six weeks you'll be good as new."

I was incredulous. Six weeks??? Intensive stretching and lifting??? I couldn't believe it. I began to complain a little.

"What do you mean, six weeks?" I argued. "I've had little aches like this my whole athletic career. I'd rest a day or two and they'd be gone."

"How old are you?" he asked.

"Twenty-six," I answered, which was my age at that time and a long time ago it was.

He made a slightly humorous puffing sound, and exclaimed, "There you are. You're not eighteen any more, are you?"

"I'm *only* twenty-six," I reiterated, a little louder than was necessary, as if he hadn't heard me correctly the first time.

"Exactly—that's why you have to lift and stretch, because you're not eighteen any more. When you're eighteen, your body is flexible, it regenerates itself, it heals itself. But at twenty-six, it's a whole new ball game."

He then launched into a lecture about how the body was only built to live thirty years, anyway, and I'd soon be on borrowed time, and if I wanted to keep exercising and being active, I would do well to start paying a little more attention to the details of caring for myself.

This was all a little bit shocking to me, and I still resisted.

"Is this how you talk to Jim Palmer?" I asked, referring to the then thirty-something All-Star Oriole pitcher.

Dr. Mathews was quick to reply, "Jim Palmer is a different species of human from you and me," he told me. "He still has the body of an eighteen year old. If you were Jim Palmer, I'd tell you to take a week off. But you're not, you're a normal human being. So if you want to keep running, you will have to stretch and lift weights. Remember: stretch and lift weights."

It was pretty clear I was being dismissed, and I dutifully left. I did do my stretches and lifting for nearly two months and I did feel as good as new—physically, at least. Dr. Mathews *had* succeeded in denting my psychological profile just a bit.

But the lesson lives on. If you want something to work, then stretch and lift weights. Using drama will be a stretch for many educators. It was for me. And yet, with the proper care and attention to detail, it will work. And I predict that it will not just work: it will work magic—the magic of true teaching and learning.

Bibliography

Works Cited

Aiken, W. 1941. *The Story of the Eight Year Study*. New York: Harper and Row.

Anderson, R.C. 1984. "Role of the Reader's Schema in Comprehension, Learning, and Memory." In *Learning to read in American schools: Basal Readers and Content Texts*. Edited by R.C. Anderson, J. Osborn, and R.J. Tierney (pp. 243–58). Hillsdale, NJ: Lawrence Erlbaum Associates.

Bakhtin, M.M. 1986. Translated by Vern McGee. *Speech Genres and Other Late Essays*. Austin: University of Texas Press.

Bakhtin, M.M. 1984. Edited and translated by Caryl Emerson. *Problems of Dosteovsky's Poetics*. Minneapolis: University of Minnesota Press.

Ball, D. 1983. *Backwards and Forwards. A technical manual for Reading Plays*. Carbondale: Southern Illinois University Press.

Banks, J.A. 1993. The Canon Debate, Knowledge Construction, and Multicultural Education. *Educational Researcher.* 22:4–14.

Barnes, D. 1986. *Language, the Learner, and the School*. London: Routledge.

Barthes, R. 1986. Translated by S. Heath. *Image–Music–Text*. New York: Hill and Wang.

Beane, J.A. 1975. "The Case for Core in the Middle School." *Middle School Journal.* 6: 33–4.

———. 1980. "The General Education We Need." *Educational Leadership.* 37: 307–8.

———. 1990. *A Middle School Curriculum: From Rhetoric to Reality.* Columbus, OH: National Middle School Association (NMSA).

———. 1993. *Affect in the Curriculum: Toward Democracy, Dignity, and Diversity.* New York: Teachers College Press.

Belcher, T. 1981. *Mental imagery in basal manuals.* Unpublished manuscript. University of Maryland: College Park.

Benton, M. 1983. "Secondary Worlds" *Journal of Research and Development in Education.* 16: 68–75.

Bigelow, B. et al (eds). 1991. *Rethinking Columbus.* Milwaukee, WI: Rethinking Schools.

Bigelow, B. Editor, *Rethinking Schools.* 1992. Special Issue on Rethinking Columbus.

Blunt, J. 1978. "Response to Reading: How Some Young Readers Describe the Process." *English in Education.* 11: 34–47.

Bolton, G. 1979. *Towards a Theory of Drama in Education.* London: Longman.

Booth, D. 1985. "Imaginary Gardens with Real Toads" In *Theory Into Practice, 24(3),* pp. 193–8. Columbus, OH: The Ohio State University.

———. 1987. *Drama Words: The role of drama in language growth.* Toronto: The Language Study Center.

———. 1995. *Story Drama.* Markham, Ontario: Pembroke.

Booth, D. and Lundy, C. 1985. *Improvisation: Learning through Drama.* Toronto: Academic Press.

Bransford, J. 1979. *Human Cognition: Learning, Understanding, and Remembering.* Belmont, CA: Wadsworth.

Brazee, E. and Capelluti, J. 1995. *Dissolving Boundaries: Toward an Integrative Curriculum.* Columbus, OH: National Middle School Association.

British Broadcasting Company. 1971. *Three Looms Waiting: The Drama Teaching of Dorothy Heathcote.* Broadcasting House: London.

Britton, J. 1984. "Message and Text in Poetic Utterance." In *Changing English: Essays for Harold Rosen.* Edited by M. Meek and J. Miller (pp. 220–35). London: Heinemann.

Brown, J., Collins, A. and DuGuid, P. 1989. "Situated Cognition and the Culture of Learning." *Educational Researcher.* 18: 32–42.

Bruner, J. 1983. *Child's Talk: Learning to Use Language.* New York: W.W. Norton.

———. 1986. *Actual Minds, Possible Worlds.* Cambridge: Harvard University Press.

Carver, S., Lehrer, R., Connell, T. and Erickson, J. 1992. "Learning by

Hypermedia Design: Issues of Assessment and Implementation." *Educational Psychologist.* 27: 385–404.

Cazden, C.B. January 1987, "Text and Context in Education." Paper presented at the Third Intenational Conference on Thinking. Honolulu, Hawaii.

Chenfeld, M. 1983 *Creative Activities for Young Children.* Yew York: Harcourt, Brace, Jovanovich.

———. 1987. (2nd ed.). *Teaching Language Arts Creatively.* San Diego: Harcourt Brace Jovanovich.

———. 1993. *Teaching is the Key of Life.* Washington DC: National Association for the Education of Young Children.

Clark, C. and Moss, P. 1996. Researching *With*: Ethical and Epistemological Implications of Doing Collaborative, Change-oriented Research with Teachers and Students. *Teachers College Record.* 97:4; 518–548.

Coe, M. 1993. Students as Researchers. *Teaching and Change,* 1: 98–107.

Conant, S., Budoff, M., and Hecht, B. 1983. *Language intervention: A communication games approach.* Cambridge, MA: Brookline books.

Connelly, F.M. and Clandinin, D.J. 1990. "Stories of Experience and Narrative Inquiry." *Educational Researcher,* 19: 2–14.

Cromer, W. 1970. "The Difference Model: A New Explanation for Some Reading Difficulties." *Journal of Educational Psychology.* 61: 471–83.

Daneman, M., and Carpenter, P. 1980. "Individual Differences in Working Memory and Reading." *Journal of Verbal Learning and Verbal Behavior.* 19: 450–56.

Delpit, L. 1993. The Silenced Dialogue: Power and Pedagogy in Educating Other People's Children. In *Beyond Silence Voices: Class, Race, and Gender in United States Schools.* Edited by L. Weis and M. Fine. Albany, NY: State University of New York Press. (pp. 119–142.)

Dewey, J. 1910. *How We Think.* Boston: Heath.

———. 1922. *The Nature of Aims.* In *John Dewey on Education: Selected Writings.* Edited by Archambauult, R.D. Chicago: University of Chicago Press.

Durkin, D. 1979. What Classroom Observations Reveal About Reading Comprehension Instruction." *Reading Research Quarterly.* 14: 481–533.

Eco, U. 1978. *The Role of the Reader.* Bloomington, IN: Indiana University Press.

Edmiston, B. 1991a. *What have you travelled? A Teacher Researcher Study of Structuring Drama for Reflection.* Doctoral dissertation, The Ohio State University, Columbus, OH.

———. 1991b. Planning for Flexibility: The Phases of a Drama Structure. *Drama/Theatre Teacher 4(1).* 6–11. Autumn.

————. 1993. Going up the Beanstalk: Discovering Giant Possibilities for Responding to Literature through Drama. In *Journeying: Children Responding to Literature.* Edited by Holland, K., Hungerford, R. & Ernest, S. B. Portsmouth, NH: Heinemann.

————. 1994. "More than Talk: A Bakhtinian Perspective on Drama in Education and Change in Understanding." In *National Association for Drama in Education Journal.* (Australia) 18: 25–36.

————. 1995. Discovering Right Actions: Forging ethical positions through dialogic interactions. In *Selected Readings in Drama and Theatre Education.* Edited by Philip Taylor and Christine Hoepper. Brisbane, Australia: National Association of Drama in Education Publications.

Edmiston, B. and Wilhelm, J. 1996. "Playing in Different Keys: Notes for Action Researchers and Reflective Drama Practitioners." In *Researching Drama and Arts Education: Paradigms and Possibilities.* Edited by Philip Taylor. London: Falmer Press.

————. 1998. "Repositioning Views/Reviewing Positions: Forming Complex Understandings in Drama." In *Educational Drama and Language Arts: What Research Shows.* Edited by B.J. Wagner. Portsmouth, NH: Heinemann.

Enciso, P. [Edmiston]. 1990. *"The Nature of Engagement in Reading: Profiles of Three Fifth Graders Engagement Strategies and Stances."* Doctoral dissertation, The Ohio State University, Columbus, OH.

————. December, 1992. *Accounting for engagement: Emerging principles for rethinking reading processes.* Paper presented at the annual conference of The National Reading Conference, San Antonio, TX.

————. December, 1994. "Teaching for the Strongest Self." Roundtable presentation at National Reading Conference, San Antonio.

————. 1996. Why Engagement in Reading Matters to Molly. *Reading and Writing Quarterly: Overcoming Learning Difficulties.* 12:171–194.

Ely, M., with Anzul, M., T. Friedman, and D. Garner, 1991. *Doing Qualitative Research: Circles Within Circles.* London, New York, and Philadelphia: The Falmer Press.

Fine, M. 1995. *Habits of Mind.* San Francisco: Jossey-Bass.

Fines, J. and Verrier, R. 1974. *The drama of history.* London: Clive Bingley.

Forman, E. and Cazden, C. 198). "Exploring Vygotskian Perspectives in Education: The Cognitive Value of Peer Interaction." In *Culture, communication, and cognition: Vygotskian perspectives.* Edited by J.V. Wertsch. pp. 323–47. New York: Cambridge University Press.

Fullan, M. and Pomfret, A. 1977. Research on Curriculum and Instructional Implementation." *Review of Educational Leadership.* 47: 335–97.

Gallas, K. 1994. *The Languages of Learning.* New York: Teachers College Press.

Gambrell, L. and Bales, R.J. 1986. Mental Imagery and the Comprehension—Monitoring Performance of Fourth and Fifth Grade Readers." *Reading Research Quarterly.* 21: 454–64.

Gambrell, L.B.and Heathington, B.S. 1981. "Adult Disabled Readers' Metacognitive Awareness about Reading Tasks and Strategies." *Journal of Reading Behavior.* 13: 215–22.

Gardner, H. 1982. *Art, Mind and Brain.* New York: Basic Books.

———. 1983. *Frames of Mind.* New York: Basic Books.

Gaskill, W. 1980. "Working with Actors." In *Exploring Theatre and Education.* Edited by K. Robinson London: Heinemann.

Geertz, C. 1973. *The Interpretations of Cultures.* New York: Basic Books.

Gilligan, C. 1982. *In a Different Voice.* Cambridge, MA: Harvard University Press.

Goodlad, J. 1984. *A Place Called School.* New York: McGraw-Hill.

Goodman, K. 1985. "Unity in Reading." In Theoretical Processes and Models of Reading, 3d edition. Edited by H. Singer and R.B. Ruddell. (pp. 813–40). Newark, DE: International Reading Association.

Greene, M. 1988. *The Dialectic of Freedom.* New York: Teachers College Press.

———. 1990. *Ethical Issues and Research.* Paper presented, The Ohio State University. Columbus, Ohio.

———. 1995. *Releasing the Imagination: Essays on Education, the Arts, and Social Change.* San Francisco: Jossey-Bass Publishers.

Guskey, T.R. 1986. "Staff Development and the Process of Teacher Change." *Educational Researcher.* 15: 5–12.

Hammersley, M. and Atkinson P. 1983. *Ethnography: Principles and Practice.* London: Tavistock.

Hansen, J. 1981. "The Effects of Inference Training and Practice on Young Children's Reading Comprehension." *Reading Research Quarterly.* 16: 391–417.

Harding, D.W. 1937, 1962. What Happens When We Read. *British Journal of Aesthetics.* 2(2).

Hardy, B. 1977. "Towards a Poetics of Fiction." In *The Cool Web.* Edited by M. Meek et al. London: The Bodley Head.

Heath, S.B. and McLaughlin, M.W. 1993. *Identity and Inner-city Youth. Beyond Ethnicity and Gender.* New York: Teacher College Press.

Heathcote, D. 1978. Of These Seeds Becoming: Drama in Education. *Educational Drama for Today's Schools.* Edited by R. B. Dhuman, Metuchen, N.J. and London: The Scarecrow Press.

————. 1982. *Heathcote at the National: Drama Teacher—Facilitator or Manipulator?* Edited by T. Goode, Banbury, Oxon: Kemble Press.

Heathcote, D., Johnson, L. and O'Neill, C., eds. 1984. *Dorothy Heathcote: Collected Writings on Education and Drama.* London: Hutchinson.

Heathcote, D. and Bolton, G. 1995. *Drama for Learning: Dorothy Heathcote's Mantle of the Expert Approach for Teaching Drama.* Portsmouth, NH: Heinemann.

Hoetker, J. and Ahlbrand, W. 1969. *"The Persistence of Recitation."* American *Educational Research Quarterly.* 6:145–67.

Iser, W. 1978. *The Act of Reading: A Theory of Aesthetic Response.* Baltimore, MD: Johns Hopkins University Press.

Janvier, C. 1987. Representation and Understanding: "The Notion of Function as an Example." In *Problems of Representation in the Teaching and Learning of Mathematics.* Edited by C. Janvier. (pp. 67–81). Hillsdale, NJ: Lawrence Erlbaum Associates.

Johnston, P. 1993. Assessment and Literate Development. *The Reading Teacher.* 46: 428–29.

Johnston, P. and Winograd, P. (December, 1983). "Passive Failure in Reading." Paper presented at the annual meeting of the National Reading Conference, Austin, TX.

Jordan, C. 1981a. "Educationally Effective Ethnology: A Study of the Contributions of Cultural Knowledge to Effective Education for Minority Children." Doctoral Dissertation, University of California, Los Angeles (available on microfilm from University Microfilms Library Services, Ann Arbor, MI).

————. 1981b. "The Selection of Culturally Compatible Teaching Practices. *Educational Perspectives.* 20: 16–19.

Kemmis, S. and McTaggart, R. 1982. *The Action Research Reader.* Geelong, Australia: Deakin University Press.

Knapp, M., Stearns, M., John, M. and Zucker, A. 1988. "Prospects for Improving K–12 Science Education from the Federal Level. *Phi Delta Kappan.* 69: 677–83.

Knoblauch, C. and Brannon, L. 1993. *Critical Teaching and the Idea of Literacy.* Portsmouth, NH: Heinemann.

Kohl H. 1994. The Politics of Children's Literature. In *Rethinking Our Classrooms.* Milwaukee, WI: Rethinking Schools.

Langer, J. 1984. Examining Background Information and Text Comprehension. *Reading Research Quarterly.* 19: 468–81.

————. 1990. "The Process of Understanding: Reading for Literary and Informational Purposes." *Research in the Teaching of English.* 24: 229–60.

Langer, S. 1953. *Feeling and Form.* New York: Scribner's.

Lave, J. and Wenger, E. 1991. *Situated Learning: Legitimate Peripheral Participation*. Cambridge and New York: Cambridge University Press.

Lemke, J.L. 1982. *Classroom Communication of Science: Final Report (SEDR-79-18961)*. Washington DC: National Science Foundation. (ERIC Document Reproduction Service No. ED 222 346).

Lehrer, R. April, 1991. "Knowledge Design in History." Paper presented at the annual meeting of American Educational Research Association, Chicago, IL.

———. 1993. Authors of Knowledge: Patterns of Hypermedia Design. In *Computers as Cognitive Tools*. Edited by S. Lajoie and S. Derry. (pp. 197–227). Hillsdale, NJ: Lawrence Erlbaum Associates.

Lehrer, R., Erickson, J. and Connell, T. 1991. Learning by Designing Hypermedia Documents. *Computers in the Schools*, 10: 227–54.

Lounsbury, J. "Six Trends to Take Us into the 21st Century." Keynote delivered at the Maine Middle Level Education Institute. University of Maine at Orono. July 10, 1996.

Lounsbury, J. and Vars, G. 1978. *A Curriculum for the Middle School Years*. New York: Harper and Row.

Miner, H. 1956. "Body Ritual among the Nacirema." *The American Anthropologist*. 58: 503–07.

Moffet, J. and Wagner, B.J. 1984. *A Student-Centered Language Arts Curriculum, K–13*. Boston: Houghton-Mifflin.

Morson, G. and Emerson, C. 1990. *Mikhail Bakhtin: Creation of a Prosaics*. Stanford, CA: Stanford University Press.

National Assessment of Educational Progress. 1981. *Three National Assessments of Reading: Changes in Performance*, 1970–1980. ED200898.

Noddings, N. 1984. *Caring: A Feminine Approach to Ethics and Moral Education*. Berkeley, CA: University of California Press.

Oldfather, P. 1993. What students say about motivating experiences in a whole language classroom. *Reading Teacher* 46: 672–681.

O'Neill, C. 1988. "Ways of Seeing: Audience Function in Drama and Theatre. In *National Association for Drama in Education Journal* (Australia). (13)

———. 1995. *Drama Worlds*. Portsmouth, NH: Heinemann.

O'Neill, C. & Lambert, A. 1982. *Drama Structures: A Practical Handbook for Teachers*. Portsmouth, NH: Heinemann.

O'Neill, C., Lambert, A., et al. 1976. *Drama Guidelines*. London: Heinemann Educational Books.

Perfetti, C.A. and Lesgold, A.M. 1979. "Coding and Comprehension in Skilled Reading and Implications for Instruction." In *Cognitive Processes in Comprehension*. Edited by L. B. Resnick and P. A. Weaver (pp. 141–83). Hillsdale: Lawrence Erlbaum Associates.

Perkins, D.N. 1986. *Knowledge as Design*. Hillsdale, NJ: Lawrence Erlbaum Associates.

———. 1988. "Art as Understanding." In *Art, Mind and Education*. Edited by H. Gardner and D. Perkins. Champaign, IL: University of Illinois Press.

Postman, N. 1995. *The End of Education*. New York: Basic Books.

Purcell–Gates, V. 1991. "On the Outside Looking in: A Study of Remedial–Readers Meaning–Making while Reading Literature." *Journal of Reading Behavior*. 23: 235–54.

Rabinow, P. (Ed.). 1984. *The Foucault Reader*. New York: Pantheon Books.

Rabinowitz, P. 1987. *Before Reading*. Ithaca, NY: Cornell University Press.

Reid, D.K. 1988. *Teaching the Learning Disabled: A Cognitive, Developmental Approach*. Boston: Allyn and Bacon.

Rosenblatt, L. 1978. *The Reader, the Text, the Poem: the Transactional Theory of the Literary Work*. Carbondale, IL: Southern Illinois University Press.

Rosenholtz, S. 1986. "Career Ladders and Merit Pay: Capricious Fads or Fundamental Reforms?" *Elementary School Journal*. 86: 513–29.

Sarason, S. 1983. *Schooling in America: Scapegoat and Salvation*. New York: Free Press.

Schank, R. 1990. *Tell Me a Story*. New York: Scribners.

Scholes, R. 1985. *Textual Power*. New Haven: Yale University Press.

Schon, D. 1983. *The Reflective Practitioner: How Professionals Think in Action*. New York: Basic Books.

Sherman, R. and Webb, R. 1988. *Qualitative Research in Education: Focus and Methods*. London: Falmer Press.

Siks, G. 1983. *Creative Dramatics*. New York: Appleton.

Singer, P., ed. 1991. *A Companion to Ethics*. London: Blackwell Reference.

Smagorinsky, P. and Coppock, J. 1995. Reading through the Lines: An Exploration of Drama as a Response to Literature. *Reading and Writing Quarterly*. 11: 369–91.

Smith, F. 1978. *Understanding Reading: A Psycholinguistic Analysis of Reading and Learning to Read*. 2nd ed. New York: Holt, Rinehart and Winston.

Smith, F. 1988. *Joining the Literacy Club: Further Essays into Education*. Portsmouth, NH: Heinemann.

Smith, M. 1992. "Submission Versus Control in Literary Transactions. In *Reader Stance and Literary Understanding: Exploring the Theories, Research and Practice*. Edited by J. Many and C. Cox Norwood, NJ: Ablex.

Spiedel, G. 1987. Conversation and Language Learning in the Classroom. In *Child Language*, Vol. 6. Edited by K. E. Nelson and A. van Kleeck. Hillsdale, NJ: Lawrence Erlbaum Associates.

Spolin, V. 1963. *Improvisation for the Theater.* Evanston, IL: Northwestern University Press

States, B. O. 1985. *Great Reckonings in Little Rooms: On the Phenomenology of Theater.* Berkeley, Los Angeles & London: University of California Press.

Stevenson, C. 1986. *Teachers as Inquirers: Strategies for Learning with and about Early Adolescents.* Columbus, OH: National Middle School Association.

Tannen, D. "Triumph of the Yell." *New York Times.* Op-ed. January 14, 1994.

Taylor, P. (Ed.). 1996. *Researching Drama and Arts Education: Paradigms and Possibilities.* New York and London: Falmer Press.

Tharp, R. and Gallimore, R.1988. *Rousing Minds to Life.* Cambridge: Cambridge University Press.

Thomson, J. 1987. *Understanding Teenagers' Reading: Reading Processes and the Teaching of Literature.* Maryborough: AATE.

Van Mannen, M. 1990. *Researching Lived Experience.* Albany, New York: State University of New York Press.

Vars, G. 1992. *A Bibliography of Research on the Effectiveness of Block-Time, Core, and Interdisciplinary Team Teaching Programs.* Unpublished manuscript: Kent State University, Kent, OH.

Vogt, L. 1985. *Training for Responsive Teaching.* Kamehaha Schools/Bishop Estate, Center for Development of Early Education.

Vygotsky, L. 1962. *Thought and Language.* Cambridge, MA: MIT Press.

———. 1978. *Mind in Society: The Development of Higher Psychological Processes.* Cambridge, MA: Harvard University Press.

Wade, S. 1983. A Synthesis of the Research for Improving Research in Social Sciences. *Review of Educational Research.* 53: 461–79.

Wagner, B.J. 1983. The expanding circle of informal classroom drama. In *Integrating the Language Arts in the Elementary School.* Edited by B.A. Bushing and J.D. Schwartz (pp. 155–63). Champaign-Urbana, IL: National Council of Teachers of English.

Wells, G. and Chang-Wells, G.L. 1992. *Constructing Knowledge Together.* Portsmouth, NH: Heinemann.

Wertsch, J. 1979. From Social Interaction to Higher Psychological Process: A Clarification and Application of Vygotsky's Theory. *Human Development.* 22: 1–22.

White, H. 1981. The value of narrativity in the representation of reality. In *On narrative.* Edited by W. J. T. Mitchell (pp. 1-24.) Chicago: The University of Chicago Press.

Wiggins, G. 1989. "Teaching to the (Authentic) Test." *Educational Leadership.* 9: 41–47.

Wilhelm, J. 1992. "Literary Theorists, Hear My Cry." *English Journal.* 81: 50–56.

———. 1995. "Creating the Missing Link: Teaching with Hypermedia." *English Journal.* 82: 34–40.

———. 1995. "Reading Is Seeing: Using Visual Response to Improve the Literary Reading of Reluctant Readers." *Journal of Reading Behavior.* 27: 467–503.

———. 1996. *Standards in Practice, Grades 6–8.* Champaign-Urbana, IL: National Council of Teachers of English.

———. 1997. *You Gotta Be the Book: Teaching Engaged and Reflective Reading with Adolescents.* New York: Teachers College Press.

Wilhelm, J. and Edmiston, B. 1998. Drama and doing the right thing. *Journal of Research in Rural Education.* 13:1–11.

Wilhelm, J. and Friedemann, P. 1998. *Hyperlearning: Teaching with Technology.* York, ME: Stenhouse.

Wolf, S., Edmiston, B. and Enciso, P. (1996). Drama worlds: "Places of the Heart, Hand, Voice and Head in Dramatic Interpretation." In *The Handbook for Literacy Educators: Research on Teaching the Communicative and Visual Arts.* Edited by J. Flood, D. Lapp, and S. B. Heath.

Wood, D. 1980. Teaching the Young Child: Some Relationships between Social Interaction, Language and Thought. In *The social foundations of language and thought.* Edited by R. Olson. (pp. 208–296.) New York: W.W. Norton.

Woods, M.L. and Moe, A.J. 1989. *Analytical Reading Inventory,* 4th ed. Columbus, OH: Merrill.

Literary Works

Bell, Derek. 1992. *Faces at the Bottom of the Well: The Permanence of Racism in America.* New York: Basic Books.

Brecht, Bertold 1963. *Mother Courage and her Children.* New York: Samuel French.

Chatwin, Bruce 1987. *The Songlines.* New York: Viking.

Dorris, Michael. 1992. *Morning Girl.* New York: Hyperion.

Jacobs, F. 1992. *The Tainos: The People Who Welcomed Columbus.* New York: Putnam.

Levinson, N. 1990. *Christopher Columbus.* New York: Lodestar/Dutton.

Lewis, Barbara. 1991. *The Kid's Guide to Social Action: How to Solve the Social Problems You Choose—and Turn Creative Thinking into Positive Action.* Minneapolis: Free Spirit.

Macaulay, David. 1977. *Castle*. Boston: Houghton-Mifflin.

Marshall, James V. 1984. *Walkabout*. New York: Sundance.

McDaniel, Lurlene. 1991 *Somewhere Between Life and Death*. New York: Starfire BDD.

Meltzer, Milton. 1990. *Columbus and the World Around Him*. New York: Franklin Watts.

Porter, Connie 1993. *Meet Addy*. Middleton, WI: Pleasant Co.

Roop, Peter and Roop, Connie 1992. *I, Columbus: My Journal*. New York: Walker and Co.

Steinbeck, John. 1939. *The Grapes of Wrath*. New York: The Viking Press.

Taylor, Mildred. 1976. *Roll of Thunder, Hear My Cry*. New York: Dial.

Weiss, Peter. 1966. *The Investigation; a Play.*. New York. Atheneum.

Yolen, Jane. 1992. *Encounter*. New York: Harcourt Brace Jovanovich.